Poetry weds the body to the soul, and *Sound Ideas* is a superb introduction to the manifold ways in which poets touch us to the core of our being. The neglected art of poetry, its forms and physicality, is the occasion for a journey into the musical heart of verse: the dance that makes the world go round. Professors McCarthy and Quinn, a scholar and a poet, respectively, draw on decades of experience in the classroom to explain how a line works, the function of meter and rhyme, the value of metaphor, and a host of other matters, in an engaging style. This should be required reading for anyone interested in poetry, particularly for those who hope to make poems themselves. A brilliant book.

—**CHRISTOPHER MERRILL**, POET, DIRECTOR OF THE
INTERNATIONAL WRITING PROGRAM, UNIVERSITY OF IOWA

T. S. Eliot once said that a poem tends to "realize itself first as a particular rhythm before it reaches expression in words, and that this rhythm may bring to birth the idea and image." *Sound Ideas* by Gene McCarthy and Fran Quinn suggests that if Eliot is right, then perhaps the usual methods of reading the poem on the page are not enough. As the wonderful pun in the title of their book suggests, ideas are only sound (reliable) when they are embodied in the sounds (music) words make. The study of poems, then, needs to include what this book so aptly provides: instruction in speaking and listening to words since the "sound of a word itself expresses meaning and emotion." While the opening chapters guide the reader (and teacher) through the methodology of reading by speaking—how the use of the line effects meaning and emotion; how a poem's matrix of vowels and consonants embody the poem's meaning; how rhythm is always the motion of the poem's emotional life—the latter chapters work through the more usual aspects of poetry (meter, image, metaphor, form). But throughout, the unique appeal of this book is its emphasis on how to speak and hear the poem. In the end, speaking and learning how to "hear" the poem brings the reader closer and closer to the poem's "sound ideas," that mysterious and startling moment when tongue, ear, and brain are all sounding together.

—**ROBERT CORDING**, POET, BARRETT CHAIR OF CREATIVE WRITING
AT THE COLLEGE OF THE HOLY CROSS

With its sophisticated readings conveyed in plain English and clearly organized into distinct chapters that parse the traditional fundamentals, *Sound Ideas* is full of experience, wisdom, common sense, and, most importantly, enthusiasm for literature. It is the fruit of years spent with poems and students in the classroom. Teachers and professors will find it of use in both literature and creative writing courses, as it contains enough well-chosen works to constitute something of an anthology, with examples ranging from Milton to Boland, from Tranströmer to Etheridge Knight. Students and general readers will find it bracing and refreshing, simultaneously instructive and delightful as well as a guide to wide and varied good taste.

—**ANTHONY E. WALTON**, POET, PROFESSOR AND
WRITER-IN-RESIDENCE AT BOWDOIN COLLEGE

Continued next page . . .

E ach chapter delves into a key property of language, demystifying and decoding its nuanced claims to literary power. In its combination of formal control and sensual contact, *Sound Ideas* offers poets and lovers of poetry a uniquely useful guide with which to explore the dark, silent cave of human life and the ways that each word can be a kind of sound-flare, a momentary illumination of what's permanently etched in the walls of songs that float ever-just-beyond our hearing.

—**ED PAVLIC**, SHEILE BIDDLE FORD FOUNDATION FELLOW, W. E. B. DU BOIS INSTITUTE, HARVARD UNIVERSITY

S *ound Ideas* appeals to me as a reader, as a poet, as a teacher of poetry, and as a teacher of the writing of poetry. There have been many books about poetry and the craft of poetry in the last ten years, but *Sound Ideas* stands above the others— for sheer insight and joy in its subject—in a way that compares only to Kenneth Koch's *Making Your Own Days*. Yet the subject matter of *Sound Ideas* is unique— and it is all the more praiseworthy that it focuses on what is so often neglected in the study of poetry: the life of the poem in its spoken and heard form. It seems amazing that such a book as this should even be necessary, for what is more fundamental to poetry as it has been understood for millennia than its spoken nature? And yet, today, when poems are taught as "texts" rather than poems, when poets will often read their own poems badly, when performance poetry and hip- hop have stepped in to fill the gap of our craving for the dynamic orality of verse, the need for this book is mighty and acute.

Professors McCarthy and Quinn have written a book that is readily accessible yet sophisticated—which is exactly what the sound texture of poetry is. The book is organized in familiar categories—Line, Imagery, and so on—yet each topic is presented in a fresh way, with incisive attention that merges with devotion. Elements such as pitch and tempo—vital aspects of the poem that traditional metrics are not prepared to handle—are brought to light and discussed with clarity. Furthermore, the discussions are not merely descriptive but functional and performative: poetic techniques are studied for what they *do* in a poem. The excellent chapter on Rhyme, for example, shows how rhyme's gravitational pull on our attention interacts with the complementary pull of syntax. So too, the various techniques discussed, both prosodic and rhetorical, are also brought into relation to each other, most helpfully when a certain poem or passage is illuminated in different chapters. The emphasis, ultimately, is on the whole poem, as the final chapter on Memory makes clear.

Examples of poems are well-chosen from a wide range of centuries and cultures; a person newly approaching poetry will come away with a diverse menu of poems intimately understood, and the skills to explore further. For me, *Sound Ideas* aces the final test of a poetry handbook: it makes me excited about poetry all over again.

—**WILLIAM WENTHE**, POET, PROFESSOR, DEPARTMENT OF ENGLISH, TEXAS TECH UNIVERSITY

SOUND IDEAS

Hearing and Speaking Poetry

B. Eugene McCarthy
& Fran Quinn

HOBBLEBUSH BOOKS
Brookline, New Hampshire

Composed in Adobe Arno Pro and Scala Sans at Hobblebush Books

Cover and back cover detail: Pablo Picasso
(Spain, 1881–1973); Vase, 1927
terra-cotta 28 ⅞ × 12 ⅞ inches (diam.)
Portland Museum of Art, Maine. Anonymous gift, 1985.324

Printed in the United States of America

Publisher's Cataloging-In-Publication Data
(Prepared by The Donohue Group, Inc.)

McCarthy, B. Eugene, 1934–
    Sound ideas : hearing and speaking poetry / B. Eugene McCarthy & Fran Quinn.

    p. ; cm.

    Includes bibliographical references and index.
    ISBN: 978-0-9845921-9-7

    1. Oral interpretation of poetry. 2. Poetry—Appreciation. I. Quinn, Fran, 1942– II. Title.
PN4151 .M33 2013
808.5/45   2012951552

HOBBLEBUSH BOOKS
17-A Old Milford Road
Brookline, New Hampshire 03033
www.hobblebush.com

Contents

Will you come with me?

Will you come with me?

I'm talking to you.
There is no other you.
Will you come with me?

I know you're there.
I feel you close to me.
Your hands are on the page.

I am here in the white,
in the spaces around the words.
Move closer.
Let your hands move across the page.
Press down.
Let your fingers sink in.
Let me see your hand.
I would hold your wrist.
Don't struggle with the white.
Let go.
Be willing to be lost.
Go easy
in the page.
Go
easy.

Move your ear closer.
Drop your head down.
Don't be satisfied with sight.
Hear the words.
Will you come with me?
Feel the words.
Will you come with me?
Will you come with me?

—Fran Quinn

Introduction

Poetry—Listening and Speaking

Reading a poem on a page is a different process from listening to it, and speaking that poem is yet another kind of process. Reading engages the eyes and mind. Listening requires mind and ears and often sight, as we watch the speaker. When we pick up the poem to read it aloud, our eyes see the words, and our voices and bodies also become active, and the poem begins to take on further and further dimensions beyond its state on the page.

Our intent with this book is to show ways that we can move a poem off the page, which is where we usually address a poem, and *listen* to it, *speak* it. The rationale is our belief that reading a poem for its intellectual content alone leaves much of the poem still untouched, undiscovered. Western poetry originated in orality, but has moved away from it.

Ordinarily when we read a poem quietly to ourselves we seek the intellectual meaning, and such too appears to be the practice when we either attend a class or teach a class on poetry. We two authors have, on the other hand, been exploring ways of teaching poetry with attention to reading and listening to the entire poem, as well as to memorizing and presenting poems, and we have become convinced that such an approach does greater justice to readers and to poems.

In a letter to Sylvia Plath, poet Ted Hughes neatly describes what we have in mind:

> Tonight I read Yeats aloud for about an hour, and I shall do this. An hour in the morning and an hour at night. Up to the inventing of Caxton's press, and for most people long after that, all reading was done aloud. . . . Eliot says that the best thing a

poet can do is read aloud poetry as much as he can. . . . Silent
reading only employs the parts of the brain which are used in
vision. Not all the brain. This means a silent reader's literary
sense becomes detached from the motor parts and the audio
parts of the brain which are used in reading aloud—tongue
and ear. This means that only one third of the mental compo-
nents are present in their writing or in their understanding of
reading—one third of the emotional charge. [1]

My own experience amplified this conviction that reading the page is
not enough. After teaching John Milton's *Paradise Lost* for some twenty-
five years, I had the opportunity to join a group that presents live drama-
tized readings of the books. Each of us felt we knew Milton quite well, but
each of us registered amazement at how much the books changed as we
began the process of preparing to speak the poem, and how much we were
changed when hearing others of the ensemble speak their passages. Even
Adam, whom I had thought I disliked, in Book IX, became a far richer, even
sympathetic, character when dramatized, for we heard all his words being
articulated with clarity, with emphasis and emotion. At least as important
as attending to the drama of the poem, we all realized that the poetry itself
became far more alive and richly meaningful. We simply heard a great deal
more at all levels. Not that I would give up the classroom study of Milton,
but now I know there is something more. The profound change we experi-
enced in the move from page to voice is like that one encounters when first
reading a play, and then acting in it, discovering on the stage the characters'
tensions and complexities, the enjoyment of the whole work.

If we take up the assumption that we can and should read poems aloud
and listen to them being read, questions come to mind: How do we listen
to poems? How do we speak poems? Are there good ways and bad ways—
even right ways and wrong ways—to read a poem, say, Keats's "La Belle
Dame Sans Merci," or Frost's "Stopping by Woods on a Snowy Evening," or
a favorite Shakespeare sonnet like "That time of year"? In brief, what is it
that we intend this book to add to what most texts and books about reading
poetry offer by way of direction or advice in reading?

What *happens* when we listen to poems, speak them aloud, and let them
into our bodies? How much deeper can we move into poems; how much
more can we hear through this openness? Responses to such questions

will include our assumptions about poetry and literature and art, why it matters, how much we can know of the art of poetry, how we gain meaning and increased value from reading poetry aloud.

With chapter one we make our entrance directly into poems: we start with line. A poem is made up of lines. It is thus different, and looks different on the page, from prose, which is made up of sentences and which is read by moving through the sentences and paragraphs. Our first principle about poems is to respect the integrity of the line. A poem then is not merely "broken-up prose" as some have called it. If we do respect the line as written, we realize that each line ends even though the sentence may not. A line can be a complete sentence ("Whose woods these are I think I know."); it can be a complete clause or phrase with a natural pause at the end ("He will not see me stopping here / To watch his woods fill up with snow."), or a break within a word group, as if Frost had written: "He will not see me / Stopping here to watch . . ." The line creates meaning and emphasis—and more.

Respecting the integrity of the line means we accept that the poet has written these lines in a particular form for a purpose. Speaking lines requires we make some acknowledgment of that break, usually by a kind of pause or by emphasis. Illustrating how one does this is the work of the chapter. We therefore take into account the way the lines move and what sort of expression the lines create. In this way, speaking the words directly assists our understanding of a poem. Stanzas, lines set off in groups, also create certain effects, sometimes developments, sometimes quick reversals, sometimes something else, as the poem moves toward its conclusion. In any case we hear the divisions of a poem into stanzas as expansions or alterations in meaning and feeling.

Our book moves forward step by step in the process of learning how to listen to and speak poems. One consequence of learning to hear lines is that we hear words in a fresh way; we hear their *sounds* and how their sounds contribute and change in conjunction with other sounds (chapter two). All words have sound, not only those words that imitate sound, like a "tinkling bell," for even in our everyday speech we choose words whose sound is part of our expression: "Quiet Please" means something different from "Silence!" or from "Shut Up." If sounds create meaning, we need to know how sounds do so and how they change.

We speak the lines of a poem so that our voice conveys both the distinctness of each line and the forward movement of lines, sentences, stanzas—a complete poem. Then the sounds of these words reveal the meaning and the emotion of the poem. While we may be uncertain how to discuss emotion in poems, we can, in fact, talk about emotion in ways that are concrete, not merely subjective. Our own emotions are often specific: a certain kind of anger, a distinct memory of a rocking chair. What we learn about the elements of poetry instructs us in the kinds of emotion we hear—and hearing is a physical response, not purely intellectual.

Reading, hearing, speaking lines of a poem with attention to the line and sound bring us to the question of how we realize vocally (i.e., learn to perform) the rhythm of a poem. As lines move down through stanzas and the whole poem, we feel the movement of emphasis, just as in natural speech our voices rise and fall, speed up and slow, emphasize and diminish words. Such a movement is rhythm (chapter three), emotion becoming motion. Of course, rhythm has a number of components, the relative speed, for example, of speaking lines, which we call tempo. These elements—the chapter's subheads treat tempo, pitch, and pause—are distinct elements of rhythm that are essential to our understanding if we are to listen well to poems, and if we are to speak poems so that our auditors grasp the meanings. Meter, a patterned system of accents, has its own chapter (four), for it is not identical to rhythm.

When we speak of traditional poetic terms—such as rhythm and meter, and later metaphor, symbolism, and the like (all the elements of verse which are called 'prosody')—we discuss them in relation to listening and speaking, but in addition, we wish to take them to a new level of understanding. For example, concerning meter, which marks each accented syllable equally, we want to raise the question of how we find and accent the main words in a line, and how each accent may vary in intensity through a line and the poem (an issue relevant to traditional and to free verse). We enlarge the scope of examining meter (what marking metrical patterns does and does not do) because determining the words we emphasize matters a great deal when we speak a poem. Frost's "Stopping by Woods" is a metrically regular poem, that is, the word accents fall evenly on each second syllable—"whose *woods* these *are* I *think* I *know*." But we do not stress each accented word equally. Which words do we stress more, and which less? How do we know for sure?

As we attend to these issues of tempo or pitch, we may realize there should be, at times, pauses or, more importantly, silences in verse, just as there are silences in our speech (chapter three, subhead "pause"). For silence means the words stop but meaning extends onward, as may happen at the end of a particularly memorable song. A page does not record silence. Our voices and bodies do.

In short, the poetic topics we address are selected not only because they are customary. We address them because they are essential to hearing and speaking poems.

Subjects like those mentioned above, such as imagery (chapter five), come under our purview because they matter to poetry. One could say, "Well, I do not *hear* any metaphor!" True: our ears are more apt to hear word sounds and rhythms. But in a real sense we do hear figurative language—like imagery, metaphor, simile—because we listen in the movement of lines to both what is being expressed and how. Figurative language conveys that *what* and *how*. While we do not separately discuss imagination, it is in many ways the root of poetry and the origin of imagery, metaphor, and simile. Imagination is sometimes seen as irregular or dangerous, but it is very much part of our daily life as a way of making sense of our world, seeing similarities, comparisons, distinctions.

In chapter nine we address the topics of allegory and symbol, neither of which we exactly hear, yet we do, of course. To state the obvious: the more we hear, the more we hear. And the better we say, the more we say. We as readers need to be conscious of the development of, for instance, an allegorical story, so that we can speak it with understanding. One feature about reading aloud is that if we read without comprehension, only getting through the words, it will be immediately obvious to any listener that we are lost. Our voices are remarkable indicators of our comprehension and mastery of a poem.

The form of a poem is often thought to be the poem's external shape or pattern visible on the page. Form can also mean the internal rationale for a poem's movement. Every poem has some kind of external form, which may be invented by the poet, and each has an internal form. A sonnet has a relatively set external form, fourteen lines of a certain length, and an arrangement of rhymes. Other external forms also have relatively set forms of lines, stanzas, rhymes, such as the sestina or villanelle. Each set form, while visible externally on a page, has its own reason for being, has its distinct internal logic and emotional shape. Each makes a certain kind of statement, suited to a certain kind of emotion. That is, one writes a villanelle because one needs a villanelle; one's particular emotion wants the form of villanelle. Awareness of such forms is an important initial position to take in reading a poem because that understanding will assist our hearing and speaking. Chapter seven takes up a sampling of external forms and explores what is meant by the internal form of each, the internal rationale (sometimes called organic form) by which the meaning or emotion moves.

If these set forms have set rhyme schemes, we need to think about rhyme: chapter eight. When we talk of rhyme schemes, it is not enough, as we said, to identify the pattern, we must also look into what that pattern is doing throughout the poem. For instance, how does an AABB rhyme differ in effect from an ABAB? The amount of time we wait for the rhyme has impact upon the meaning.

The terms mentioned above are mostly traditional ones, perhaps ones we have heard before in classrooms. But while traditional and necessary for our use, they may also present the hazard of seeming too commonplace and thus to have little value. We neither wish to eliminate these terms nor let them restrict our understanding as we press deeper into poems. As was said, we wish to take poetic terms to greater levels of understanding, to expand our comprehension of the capacities of each. We also found that there is a serious need for new terminology to describe those aspects of poetry which have not received sufficient attention. In 1986, Denise Levertov pointed out, "All discussion of contemporary poetics is vitiated by the lack of a more precise terminology."[2]

The terms we introduce, such as tempo and pitch, are drawn from ordinary speech, as we strive to avoid esoteric vocabulary. The terms arise from close observation and description of what is happening in both traditional and contemporary verse forms. Our purpose in this effort is to enable readers on their own to hear and describe what they perceive to be happening in poems, borrowing to the degree needed from prescribed terminology and from our own expanded vocabulary.

Finally, we have learned that one of the most effective ways of drawing a poem into our minds and bodies is to memorize it (chapter ten). Memory directly engages reading, hearing, speaking. That is, we read, we practice hearing the poem, we practice speaking it until its rhythms, its phrasings, with its changing tempos and pauses, sound as near to the voice of the speaker as we can approximate, and the poem becomes part of our consciousness: it speaks to us physically and emotionally so that we hold in ourselves its complete intellectual and emotional meaning. With Ted Hughes, we urge reading poems aloud. In memorizing a poem, we solve as many problems in the poem as we can so we can speak it like effective natural speech. We place it in our mental bank, we speak it out vocally in the voice of the poet or poem's speaker, and our physical bodies then contain the poem in a singular manner.

Throughout, the center of our search has been the question, "How does this approach help us to understand poetry?" The impulse for our work in teaching and in writing this book has been driven by what we learned to be students' needs—and our own needs—rather than by critical-theoretical strategies. That we have taught all the poems we include here allowed us to discover many of their prosodic pleasures. Listening to a student recite a memorized poem has invariably been an illuminating experience, for whenever mistakes were made, we along with the student were obliged to solve our problems with the poem, as we both trained our ears.

The poems here were not necessarily selected as the best "examples" of simile, for instance, or iambic meter, or sound. Mostly they are poems that we like and we feel are important. With no attempt to be anthology-inclusive, we follow here a practice used in class and workshop: be eclectic; include canonical poems in order to hear them afresh; add little-known traditional and contemporary poems to challenge teacher and student.

We have discovered that our way of approaching poems is basic both for readers already knowledgeable about poetry and for readers contemplating a first venture through the door. While nothing here is difficult, we will not tag the book with a cliché like "user-friendly." We ask for an effort, because we believe that poems deserve our attention and richly reward it, making us attentive and receptive humans. With this *vade mecum* in hand, wherever we go in poetry the principles espoused here will continue to be valid, will assist us in hearing more in each poem than we may have expected, will direct us in further reading, study, and enjoyment—writing, too, for that matter. Our work on poetry has been most exciting and fruitful when in the company of an audience—each other, twenty-five undergraduates, or . . . you.

The two of us who made this book are both teachers, most of our years at college and university level, and some at high school. One of us is a poet, the other a scholar (these terms are descriptive, not claims of authority). Though this book was not co-written in the sense that each of us authored

half, it has been conceptually, and actually, a joint project from the begin-
ning of our work together. The idea of reading poetry in the ways we discuss
here grew from a series of team-taught, first-year college poetry courses,
from teaching poetry at various collegiate levels on our own, from teaching
poetry workshops, and from literally endless discussions and arguments,
drinking coffee in diners, sitting in offices, and talking on the phone. Our
understanding has been enhanced by the experience of Quinn's poetry
workshops in New York, Indianapolis, Los Angeles, and Boston. In the
midst of New England winters, our discussions were a guaranteed source
of friction and heat, and finally light.

1. Ted Hughes, *Letters of Ted Hughes*, Selected and Edited by Christopher Reid. New
   York: Farrar and Giroux, 1956, 50.
2. Denise Levertov, "On the Need for New Terms," *New & Selected Essays*, New York:
   New Direction Books, 1992, 74.

SOUND IDEAS

Chapter One

Line

When we see poems on a page, they normally appear in the form of lines. A line of verse may be made up of a complete sentence, or it can be part of a sentence, a clause, a phrase, or a part of a word group, for example, a preposition separated from its object. Poems are written in lines because lines can be used for a wide variety of effects, so we begin the process of listening to and speaking poems by examining what these effects are, what line does.

At the very least, breaking a sentence into lines is a way to achieve emphasis. In order to make a point in ordinary speech we might say, "I wish you would not do that!" Our tone of voice and gestures ensure emphasis on the right words. But on the page the words do not show emphasis. In verse we use line to create expression. If we were to write,

> I wish you would not
> do that!

stress falls on "do" because the space, break, or pause after "would not" sets up emphasis on "do that." If we change the line, we change the emphasis.

We begin with line because it is an essential element of verse, and the way we hear and say the line shapes meaning. The line is a unit in itself, whether or not it is a complete sentence. We read the line with attention, and at its end we pause to some degree even when the syntax runs to the next line. Our principle is: *respect the integrity of the line as written.*

Because the word *verse* meant originally a *turn* (as in *reverse*) at the end of a line, there is an expectation of a turning, a going back, as well as a continuation to the next line, the turn often marked by a kind of pause. The idea of *verse* as *turn* has been at times imaged as the movement of a dancer, stepping across the stage or platform, then pausing before returning. We are aware that in staged Greek verse, the movement and pause of dancers coincided with those of the line.[1] The term *verse* can also suggest the action of a plowman, advancing across a field, then turning at the end of a furrow to head back. Whatever its early senses, verse continues to mean a turn, thus a pausing to denote that feel of turning, continuing to something more. So line suggests a physical movement forward. When speaking verse we acknowledge the turning at the end of the line with a vocal mark, a pause, an emphasis. How that turn can be recognized and vocalized is our concern here.

The first poem we discuss could well stand as the title of this chapter, for it is about hearing the movement of line. Here is Robert Francis's "The Sound I Listened For":

> What I remember is the ebb and flow of sound
> That summer morning as the mower came and went
> And came again, crescendo and diminuendo,
> And always when the sound was loudest how it ceased
> A moment while he backed the horses for the turn,
> The rapid clatter giving place to the slow click
> And the mower's voice. That was the sound I listened for.
> The voice did what the horses did. It shared the action
> As sympathetic magic does or incantation.
> The voice hauled and the horses hauled. The strength of one
> Was in the other and in the strength was no impatience.
> Over and over as the mower made his rounds
> I heard his voice and only once or twice he backed
> And turned and went ahead and spoke no word at all.

The first line, which draws attention to "the ebb and flow of sound," would seem to be a complete sentence, so we are inclined to pause before turning to learn when the sound took place. But the sentence continues to move (for six and a half lines) so we need to pause but not break the movement of the sentence. While Francis's lines lead us forward, each line end has a distinct and different break. In line two "as the mower came and went / And came again," our slight pause at "and went" slows the mower's action before the change and return, "And came again." The pause at the end of line four is different again because it breaks the verb from adverb: "how it ceased / A moment while he backed . . ." If we do not "cease," we do not hear the moment of cessation, an important dramatizing of the mower's movement.

As Francis's poem comes off the page, we hear how he uses line to shape action and meaning, and we hear the speaker's attention to the action. By means of line (and other verse elements we will come to later), Francis unifies the man and the action, the strength and command of voice with the response of the horses. The sound of the mower's voice is harmonized with the sound of the mechanism, just as my listener's attention is to the man, voice, action, and turn. If "The strength of one / Was in the other and in the strength was no impatience," we understand that the plowman's voice was not contrived but natural, coherent with his horses and his work: "it ceased / A moment." Even at "he backed / And turned and went ahead . . ." there is a physical pause during which he "spoke no word at all." We not only pause at line break, we pause *differently* at each, depending on the way the line prepares us for the next line.

While lines can be of similar length (Francis's are twelve syllables each) or irregular, line breaks occur in order to create voice expression. Take an example: "I don't care what you want." What the sentence means is clear on the page. But the precise vocal emphasis, tone, and emotion remain indefinite. Introducing a line break isolates a word to throw emphasis on it. We can compare these variations:

> I don't care what
> you want.

> I don't care what you
> want.

> I don't care
> what you want.

Each has the same informational meaning—but very different emotional meaning. Each line break changes the pause and emphasis, and thus makes possible this flexible emphasis in verse—and of course creates a good deal more, such as rhythm.

A line break, then, is an interruption in the movement of the speaker's voice; the voice hesitates, but it also goes on. As we say "I don't care what," the energy of the voice does not drop but holds at "what" and prepares for the next line: "you want." The interruption anticipates what is to come. Silence—a distinct break—can also be articulate. Consider what unmistakable meaning is conveyed in these contrary line-break silences:

> I want to be with you
> forever
>
> I do not want to see you
> ever

If we notice that, in these examples, the voice does not respond the way it did in "I don't care what / you want," or in the earlier "I wish you would not / do that!" we already see there can be no dogmatic rule on line break and pause; more needs to be explored as we go along.

We say that poetry is the art of the line. Prose, on the other hand, is the art of the sentence. While neither definition is absolute—there are prose poems—both point to essential distinctions. The rhythm of verse is not unnatural. In fact, our speech is often closer to verse rhythms than to prose statements. That is, our speech is based on rhythms of phrasing, emphasizing, pausing, quickening and slowing, in tempos that are characteristic of the line breaks of verse. (That is not to say, of course, that the language of verse is the same as everyday speech, for verse is careful in selection, placement, and phrasing of words.) As critic Northrop Frye put it, "The language of ordinary speech . . . has a loose associative rhythm quite different from actual prose."[2] That is, the "rhythm of prose is continuous" through to the end of the sentence, whereas verse has recurrent rhythms[3] that usually correspond to the line. Prose has phrasing, of course, and varied tempo, and emphasis, but prose follows syntactic patterns of simple, compound, and complex forms, and its formality has its own distinct elongated rhythms.

Traditional and Contemporary Uses of Line

Taking a cue from the opening stanza of "Preface" by Czeslaw Milosz, in *A Treatise on Poetry*:

> First, plain speech in the mother tongue.
> Hearing it, you should be able to see

Apple trees, a river, the bend of a road,
As if in a flash of summer lightning.

We may recognize in contemporary verse the phrasing and turns of ordinary speech. Because in older traditional English verse the diction and sometimes the more complex syntax are less familiar to us—sometimes quite foreign to our ears—the expressive phrasing and pauses of, say, seventeenth-century English verse may not appear to be based on natural speech patterns. Pronouncing the words helps us overcome what may seem at times peculiar spellings. We will first discuss line use in a traditional poem to observe how the speaker's voice approximates natural speech patterns in the movement of line and line break.

In George Herbert's "Love," a remarkable conjunction of spirit and body, the lines alternate length:

Love bade me welcome: yet my soul drew back,
　　Guilty of dust and sin.
But quick-eye'd Love, observing me grow slack
　　From my first entrance in,
Drew nearer to me, sweetly questioning
　　If I lack'd anything.

"A guest," I answer'd, "worthy to be here."
　　Love said, "You shall be he."
"I, the unkind, ungrateful? Ah, my dear,
　　I cannot look on Thee."
Love took my hand and smiling did reply,
　　"Who made the eyes but I?"

"Truth, Lord; but I have marr'd them: let my shame
　　Go where it doth deserve."
"And know you not," says Love, "who bore the blame?"
　　"My dear, then I will serve."
"You must sit down," says Love, "and taste my meat."
　　So I did sit and eat.

The first line slows at "drew back" and the second ends with a period, as if the soul has little to say. But the response of "quick-eyed Love" accelerates the lines and sweeps ahead to contrast with the speaker's reluctance or failure—he falls "slack" at "entrance in," as if with sexual incapacity ("lack" echoes "slack"). While no punctuation slows us after "slack," that rhymed word surprises us as we turn to expect clarification of this slackening. The line break after "questioning" anticipates Love's sweet voice. At the end of lines 1, 3, 4, and 5 we know each sentence continues, yet the *nature* of that continuation is distinct to each line. We see/hear/feel the difference each line break makes. The turn-pause following "back" is different from that after "slack," not just on account of the comma.

Pause at line end has both *duration* and *quality*: the *length* of the pause, and the *kind* of pause indicated. The dialogue in Herbert's second and third stanzas further adds to the naturalness of speech, for each character speaks in a voice appropriate to each. To sum up our observations on line: we listen to the movement of the line; the nature or kind of its turn; the duration and quality of the pause; the nature of enjambment; and the way the turn controls and varies line speed.

A poem by William Carlos Williams in the twentieth century may seem eons distant from Herbert's from the seventeenth. Yet if our principles stand, line will have an equally crucial effect.

> *To a Poor Old Woman*
>
> munching a plum on
> the street a paper bag
> of them in her hand
>
> They taste good to her
> They taste good
> to her. They taste
> good to her
>
> You can see it by
> the way she gives herself
> to the one half
> sucked out in her hand
>
> Comforted
> a solace of ripe plums
> seeming to fill the air
> They taste good to her

The relation between sentence and line is especially marked here, for

Williams exploits that tension to create a remarkable variety of emphases, in a sensory celebration of a ragged old person. He does it in American speech patterns, the way Americans speak and phrase an experience. If we listen to the way the lines move and what emphases they make (there is minimal punctuation), we recognize not only specific details but how and why Williams brings such meticulous attention to each detail: street, bag, hand, taste. In other words, his lines lead us to experience not only *what* he says but *how* he says it, how he arranges lines to create vocal expression of her experience. Each rephrasing of "taste good to her" rings new emphasis, such as that wonderful "good" that begins line seven. The next line, "You can see it by," holds back detail so that the end-pause or turn throws an almost physical weight on "the way" (not on "gives") just as does "one half / sucked." The summing line—now enriched with multiple personal and sensory details—says it straight out: "They taste good to her."

Lines in contemporary verse are more likely than in traditional to vary in length in order to explore a range of expressive emphases and rhythms. In the opening lines of "St. Francis and the Sow," Galway Kinnell expands quickly from two to twelve syllables:

> The bud
> stands for all things,
> even those things that don't flower,
> for everything flowers, from within, of self-blessing;
> though sometimes it is necessary
> to reteach a thing its loveliness,
> to put a hand on its brow
> of the flower
> and retell it in words and in touch
> it is lovely
> until it flowers again from within, of self-blessing;
> as St. Francis
> put his hand on the creased forehead
> of the sow, and told her in words and in touch
> blessings of earth on the sow, and the sow
> began remembering all down her thick length,
> from the earthen snout all the way
> through the fodder and slops to the spiritual curl of the tail,
> from the hard spininess spiked out from the spine

down through the great broken heart
to the blue milken dreaminess spurting and shuddering
from the fourteen teats into the fourteen mouths sucking and
                             blowing beneath them:
the long, perfect loveliness of sow.

After identifying "bud," Kinnell follows with the argument: "stands for all things." Two long lines reiterate "everything" and repeat "flower" and, with the delicate "from within," run on to the triumphant "self-blessing." Lines 2 and 3 seem able to stand alone—but the next line adds a fresh dimension. The long second-last line (19 syllables) mimics the breathless sucking of the piglets.

The Effects of Line Use

To pursue the variety of ways that line creates meaning in verse, we will return to another poem of George Herbert, a master of line and stanza forms:

The Church-floor

Mark you the floor? that square and speckled stone
         Which looks so firm and strong,
              Is *Patience:*
And th'other black and grave, wherewith each one
         Is checker'd all along,
              Humility:
The gentle rising, which on either hand,
         Leads to the Choir above,
              Is *Confidence:*
But the sweet cement, which in one sure band
         Ties the whole frame, is *Love*
              And *Charity.*

    Hither sometimes Sin steals, and stains
    The marble's neat and curious veins:
But all is cleansed when the marble weeps.
    Sometimes Death, puffing at the door,
    Blows all the dust about the floor:
But while he thinks to spoil the room, he sweeps.
    Blest be the *Architect*, whose art
    Could build so strong in a weak heart.

Since we see on the page that the lines in the first four stanzas vary in length (10 to 6 to 4 syllables), we might ask what difference this makes in hearing and speaking these stanzas. Each 10 syllable line has mid-line punctuation, yet each set of lines moves differently and depends for emphasis upon the line-break pause. Each three-line group stresses important words: "stone," "firm and strong" lead to its virtue: "Is *Patience*." So too "each one / Is checkered" moves toward "*Humility*," as "hand, / Leads" move to the most important virtue, "band / Ties the whole frame, is *Love* / And *Charity*."

The second group or stanza intensifies the meditation on God's response to Sin and Death. The two 8-syllable lines on Sin and Death are counteracted by the 10-syllable line. The final pair affirms the power of God-the-architect. With a variety of quite natural sounding pauses and stresses on main words, these lines shape our phrasing and word emphasis to bring forth meaning and emotion.

Herbert illustrates how he, and any poet, enjoys the freedom to arrange lines and manipulate his forms even with lines of set length. Can a poet be as free and versatile with a fixed form, like the sonnet with its fourteen ten-syllable lines with set rhyme scheme? Here is Shakespeare's Sonnet 129:

> Th'expense of spirit in a waste of shame
> Is lust in action, and till action, lust
> Is perjured, murd'rous, bloody, full of blame,
> Savage, extreme, rude, cruel, not to trust;
> Enjoy'd no sooner but despiséd straight,
> Past reason hunted, and no sooner had,
> Past reason hated as a swallowed bait
> On purpose laid to make the taker mad:
> Mad in pursuit and in possession so,
> Had, having, and in quest to have, extreme;
> A bliss in proof, and proved, a very woe,
> Before, a joy proposed, behind, a dream.
>   All this the world well knows yet none knows well
>   To shun the heaven that leads men to this hell.

The movement of the opening line leads us to anticipate, with a slight pause, the verb and complement (which come down hard): "Is lust." Repeating "lust" at line-end prepares by pause and emphasis for the devastating list of nine adjectives: "Is perjur'd, murd'rous, bloody . . ." Word placements to end and begin lines (as well as word repetitions) are particularly dramatic in this sonnet. Throughout, in the pauses, silences, harshness, we hear the changes of emotional tension. The first quatrain ends with a period, as the second does with a colon. (Shakespeare's sonnets have three quatrains and a couplet; the first eight lines, or octet, usually set the problem, the six, or sestet, solve it or the couplet alone does.) The third quatrain's rhyme words (so–woe, extreme–dream) expose the continued extremity of passion, and the lines too are disrupted: "Mad in pursuit and in possession so, / Had, having, and in quest to have, extreme." Suddenly, the couplet that concludes the poem runs without midline breaks: the sonnet has resolved the conflict—though rhyming "well" with "hell" admits that danger persists.

Here is another of Shakespeare's sonnets, number 29:

> When in disgrace with Fortune and men's eyes,
> I all alone beweep my outcast state,
> And trouble deaf heaven with my bootless cries,
> And look upon myself and curse my fate,
> Wishing me like to one more rich in hope,
> Featured like him, like him with friends possessed,
> Desiring this man's art, and that man's scope,
> With what I most enjoy contented least;
> Yet in these thoughts myself almost despising,
> Haply I think on thee, and then my state
> (Like to the lark at break of day arising
> From sullen earth) sings hymns at heaven's gate,
>> For thy sweet love rememb'red such wealth brings
>> That then I scorn to change my state with kings.

The emotional tone of this sonnet is clearly different from "Th' expense of spirit." For one thing the lines move unbroken until six and seven, each ending with a comma. In fact, in speaking them, our speech pattern must hold out across those eight lines as a single sentence until: "Yet in these thoughts." The compound verbs help us to hold together the octet/sentence: "I beweep," "trouble," "look . . . and curse." The sestet in this poem holds the resolution, and line 11 expands into the beautiful lark image to describe "my state," the sound rising up from the morose vowels of earth: "Like to the lark at break of day arising / From sullen earth."

Though both these poems appear to be in the familiar English sonnet form of three quatrains and a couplet, to read each aloud is to hear their distinct character, the frequent pauses and hesitations in number 129, the strong drive of an entirely different emotion in 29.

One more example of the complex yet natural effects line can achieve in traditional iambic verse, John Donne's sonnet conveys quite a distinct tone of voice from the two of Shakespeare:

> At the round earth's imagined corners, blow
> Your trumpets, Angels, and arise, arise
> From death, you numberless infinities
> Of souls, and to your scattered bodies go,
> All whom the flood did, and fire shall o'erthrow,
> All whom war, dearth, age, agues, tyrannies,
> Despair, law, chance, hath slain, and you whose eyes
> Shall behold God, and never taste death's woe.
> But let them sleep, Lord, and me mourn a space,
> For, if above all these, my sins abound,
> 'Tis late to ask abundance of thy grace,
> When we are there; here on this lowly ground,
> > Teach me how to repent; for that's as good
> > As if thou hadst seal'd my pardon, with thy blood.

The grandeur of these lines is enhanced by strong pauses and changes of pace, as Donne exploits the drama of line-end words. There is no question that "blow" emphatically accentuates "Your trumpets." The pause ("Angels") before the repeated "arise" lifts our voices upward, above the low vowels and grim consonants of "From death." The "go" at line (and quatrain) end is easily elongated with wonderful emphasis as he sends souls scurrying off at the Last Judgment to reclaim their long-lost bodies. To run the lines together might not change the literal meaning. But the pause at each line-end word excites a powerful effect that generates the speaker's exuberant sense of triumph: we want to blast that "blow."

Emphasis, Meaning, and Emotion

A line break ordinarily throws emphasis on a word that ends and/or begins a line. Such is the case with Shakespeare's "shame / Is lust" and "lust / Is

perjur'd," and also with the Donne: "At the round earth's imagined cor-
ners, blow / Your trumpets, Angels, and arise, arise . . ." While the stress
on such a first or last word may not be the dominant one in the line, it
carries a degree of emphasis (more on this under meter in chapter four).
Yet when we compare Sonnet 29, the end and beginning words "eyes, / I
all alone," "state, / And trouble" seem not to receive the same impact or
volume. Words which end or begin lines that are syntactically complete,
such as phrases, clauses, or sentences, already possess a certain stress,
whereas broken syntax emphasizes other words, as in "arise / From death."
(*Syntax means sentence structure*: subject–verb; subject–verb–comple-
ment; subject–verb–object; subject–verb–indirect object–direct object;
subject–verb–object–complement.)

    John Milton was blind when he wrote his epic poem *Paradise Lost*
(1674)—a considerable trick if you think about it: no touchtype keyboard,
no tape recorder, just John and his memory and a secretary copying the
lines he recited each morning. This means that in many ways *Paradise Lost*
is an oral poem, bearing the marks of spoken-voice expression. There is,
admittedly, some hazard in our moving from short, easily encompassed
single poems to short passages from a long narrative poem. *Paradise Lost*
(in blank verse, ten-syllable unrhymed lines) is a twelve-book epic, 798 lines
in Book I alone—and we cannot pretend to treat here Milton's use of line
throughout the length of that work. Yet it can be instructive to cite select
details of a large work, as we might focus on Monet's brush strokes in only
one of his haystack series, or a single theme of a Bach fugue. We cite this
and the following examples to illustrate another way line can be used to
create meaning and emotion.

> No more of talk where God or angel guest
> With man, as with his friend, familiar used
> To sit indulgent, and with him partake
> Rural repast, permitting him the while
> Venial discourse unblamed: I now must change
> Those notes to tragic; foul distrust, and breach
> Disloyal on the part of Man, revolt,
> And disobedience: . . . (**IX**, 1–8)

The speaker's voice begins gently and the turn from "angel guest / With man"
is but slightly stressed. There continues a comfortable conversation with
good friends with little line-end break. Already, however, hints of tension

creep in, "permitting," "unblamed," as if this chat were acutely temporary. The very relaxed pace of these first lines offers a lesson: danger hovers near. We are literally halted in our voices at "must change" (a pained silence: terrible matters now arise!) and the jarring turn of "breach / Disloyal," echoed in "distrust" and "disobedience."

In a passage concerning Hell, in the first book of *Paradise Lost*, we read:

> yet from those flames
> No light, but rather darkness visible
> Serv'd only to discover sights of woe,
> Regions of sorrow, doleful shades, where peace
> And rest can never dwell, hope never comes
> That comes to all; . . . (I, 62–67)

While stress falls emphatically on "No light," "darkness visible" seems to end the clause, meaning there was not light but a tangible darkness. But when the sentence continues, the syntax adjusts to new meaning and what seemed to end the line becomes the subject of the next line's "Serv'd," stressing heavily what the darkness disclosed. The word "peace" hangs at line-end to show it is beyond Satan's reach ("peace" is not the same as "rest"), just as "hope never comes" stands at line-end for us to ponder before the crushing climax: "That comes to all"—all, that is, but Satan. In a preface to the poem, Milton explained that he intended his line to draw out the sense "from one verse into another," thereby adding thought onto thought.

In "The Prelude" (1850), William Wordsworth used the line's deliberate ten-syllable pace to enhance his conversational voice. There is not so much a full pause or stop at each line break but a stress, an assertion of emphasis which that position creates:

> Fair seed-time had my soul, and I grew up
> Fostered alike by beauty and by fear:
> Much favoured in my birth-place, and no less
> In that beloved Vale to which erelong
> We were transplanted—there were we let loose
> For sports of wider range. Ere I had told
> Ten birth-days, when among the mountain slopes
> Frost, and the breath of frosty wind . . .
> (Book 1)

The voice lifts somewhat and hesitates beautifully at "up," as it does at "less" and "loose" so that the first words of the next lines carry with their sound crucial syntactic weight, "Fostered," "Much favoured," "For sports," "Ten birth-days." The slight delay after "told" accents the certain pleasure of those "Ten birth-days."

A pause or recognition of the turn at line breaks seems almost always critical in conveying the expressive meaning of a passage, no matter the form or nature of the poem: sonnet or free verse, lyric, dramatic, or narrative. Even in passages of blank verse which enumerate factual matter, emphasis is created by line. In another long work, this time a drama, Shakespeare's King Henry V is instructing the Archbishop of Canterbury to ratify his right to invade France:

> My learned lord, we pray you to proceed
> And justly and religiously unfold
> Why the law Salic that they have in France
> Or should, or should not, bar us in our claim.
> And God forbid, my dear and faithful lord,
> That you should fashion, wrest or bow your reading,
> Or nicely charge your understanding soul
> With opening titles miscreate whose right
> Suits not in native colors with the truth.
>
> (*Henry V*, I, ii, 9–17)

The King's salutation seems to encourage the archbishop, but at the line break cautions him: "justly and religiously." Caution continues in line four's "Or should, or should not." In case the Archbishop still does not hear warnings, the King reinforces with "And God forbid, my dear and faithful lord." The line ending "bow your reading" brings ironic weight on "Or nicely charge." That "soul" at line end unsubtly reminds his auditor of religion, God, faith, and threat of damnation—not to mention regal displeasure. If one reads the passage as mere statement, Henry's carefully placed warnings are lost, his character weakened, the drama deflated.

We take a moment for clarification and some history of poetry.

When we speak of verse with so many syllables per line, we do so because we believe that syllable count matters, not because we wish to avoid traditional terms like meter or foot (which we take up in chapter four). Ten-syllable lines in English verse are typically iambic, that is, five feet (sets) of unstress–stress syllables. There are also shorter lines with, for example, four feet. (While iambic is a basic English foot, there are other feet as well; again, see chapter four.) We observe syllables-per-line because that is an instantly visible measure, and we gain a terminology for comparing longer or shorter length lines. We do not neglect the metrical foot patterns but at this point prefer not to include the issue of metrical stresses per line.

The ten-syllable blank verse line which we have been illustrating did not always exist in English verse. Poets had to develop it through experiment until they achieved a distinct verse line that suited the English language, distinct from Latin verse or Greek. Those languages would have served as natural models, but they were quantitative in form, which means that their verse rhythms were based on the long and short syllables. English does not have longs and shorts the way Latin does; it has accents on syllables. We can of course speak of long or short vowels in English but they have nothing to do with accent. The word "camera" is accented on the first syllable but none of its vowels are long. "Place" has a long "a" like the letter "a." The ten-syllable line was developed as one of the most flexible and effective vehicles for serious poems. It was used for blank verse dramas by Marlowe and Shakespeare, in comedy and tragedy and romance. (Earlier dramatists had tried a fourteen-syllable line which William Blake in the late eighteenth century turned to effective use for prophetic poems.) It was used in sonnets and (much earlier, in fact) in the closed couplet. Its rhythm was predominantly iambic: unstress–stress. This too was deemed the natural meter of English speech.

Long narrative poems are not, we might note here, unique to older traditional verse genres. Poets of all ages have composed long poems, written over many years, utilizing a rich array of versification. In modern times, one could mention as a brief sampling Ezra Pound's *The Cantos* (1925–72), William Carlos Williams's *Paterson* (1963), Charles Olson's *The Maximus Poems* (1953–75), Thomas McGrath's *Letter to an Imaginary Friend* (1962, 1985). One might be tempted to include longish works like Seamus Heaney's fifty-page "Squarings" (*Seeing Things*, 1991), but for that matter many books of poems generate a wholeness and are read as unified works.

Here is a passage from McGrath's *Letter*, Part Two, IV:

Moon in Virgo.
                    Autumn over the land,
    Its smoky light, its . . .
                        hawkhover
                            crowhover
                                its lonely distances
Taut with migrant birds and bodiless calls far—farther
Than noon will own or night
                        cloaked all in mystery of farewell.
    Morning stirring in the haymow must: sour blankets,
    Worn bindles and half-patched soogans of working bundlestiffs
    Stir:
            Morning in the swamp!
                        I kick myself awake
    And dress while around me the men curse for the end for the world.

    And it *is* ending (half-past-'29) but we don't know it
    And wake without light.
                    Twenty-odd of us—and very odd,
        Some.
                One of the last of the migrant worker crews
    On one of the last steam threshing rigs.
                            Antediluvian
    Monsters, all.
                    Rouse to the new day in the fragrant
    Barnloft soft haybeds: wise heads, gray;
    And gay cheechakos from Chicago-town; and cranky Wobblies;
    Scissorbills and homeguards and grassgreen wizards from the playing
                                                    fields
    Of the Big Ten: and decompressed bank clerks and bounty jumpers
    Jew and Gentile; and the odd Communist now and then
    To season the host.
                    Stick your head through the haymow door—
    Ah!
        A soft and backing wind: the Orient red
    East. And dull sky for the first faint light and no sun yet.

These sprawling lines are not of a regular length, like blank verse, but their span creates a wide landscape in which McGrath's natural phrasing has amplitude to stretch out; his phrasing is like natural speech,

> I kick myself awake
> And dress while around me the men curse for the end for the world.

> And it *is* ending (half-past-'29) but we don't know it
> And wake without light.

There is space to think, pause, reflect, go on, into what we know is going to be an extensive travel beyond these men into history: "(half-past-'29)."

Flexibility of Purpose in Line

A twentieth-century poet's ten-syllable verse, William Butler Yeats's "The Second Coming," opens (in the first of two stanzas) with several whole-line assertions:

> Turning and turning in the widening gyre
> The falcon cannot hear the falconer;
> Things fall apart; the center cannot hold;
> Mere anarchy is loosed upon the world,
> The blood-dimmed tide is loosed, and everywhere
> The ceremony of innocence is drowned;
> The best lack all conviction, while the worst
> Are full of passionate intensity.

The assertions intensify, some short, some line-length, as they move toward the decisive "everywhere" which drops enormous weight on the line-ending words "drowned" and "worst."

In George Mackay Brown's "Prince in the Heather," the strength of the long lines is undermined by alternating shorter lines about the Scots' bard's despair, despair at the disastrous loss at the battle of Culloden against the English in 1746:

> Who would have thought the land that we grew in, our mother,
> Would turn on us like a harlot?
> The rock where the stag stood at dawn,
> His antlers a proud script against the sky,
> Gave us no shelter.
> That April morning the long black rain
> Bogged our feet down
> But it did not douche the terrible fire of the English,
> Their spewings of flame . . .

> We prayed our endless mountain tracks
> Would baffle the hunters
> But the armies marched like doom on the one road
> To the one graveyard.

Another pair of lines is all sorrow, the sound declining abruptly:

> (I think it will rain a long time at Culloden
> And steel rot under the stone.)

By letting the dread name "Culloden" (near-rhyming with "stone") hang at the line end and in Scots' memory, the consequence of rain and time becomes more painful.

Yusef Komunyakaa, in his Vietnam war poem "Tunnels," changes the speaker's point of view from description of an action to his emotional engagement with a fellow soldier. The poem begins:

> Crawling down headfirst into the hole,
> he kicks the air & disappears.
> I feel like I'm down there
> with him, moving ahead, pushed
> by a river of darkness, feeling
> blessed for each inch of the unknown.
> Our tunnel rat is the smallest man
> in the platoon, in an echo chamber
> that makes his ears bleed
> when he pulls the trigger.
> He moves as if trying to outdo
> blind fish easing toward imagined blue,
> pulled by something greater than life's
> ambitions. He can't think about
> spiders & scorpions mending the air,
> or care about bats upside down
> like gods in the mole's blackness.
> The damp smell goes deeper
> than the stench of honey buckets.
> A web of booby traps waits, ready
> to spring into broken stars.
> Forced onward by some need,

some urge, he knows the pulse
of mysteries & diversions
like thoughts trapped in the ground.
He questions each root.
Every cornered shadow has a life
to bargain with. Like an angel
pushed up against what hurts,
his globe-shaped helmet
follows the gold ring his flashlight
casts into the void. Through silver
lice, shit, maggots, & vapor of pestilence,
he goes, the good soldier,
on hands & knees, tunneling past
death sacked into a blind corner,
loving the weight of the shotgun
that will someday dig his grave.

As the speaker watches his buddy's descent, his sympathy becomes claustrophobic and at each line-end he hesitates a little: "down there / with him," the line itself hesitant, "moving ahead, pushed / by a river of darkness, feeling / blessed for each inch." Pulling back a moment with seeming discompassion (line 7), the speaker prepares for the shock at the tunnel rat's ears bleeding . . . from his own gun's blast. The speaker's breathlessness (like the soldier's) increases inside the expanding underwater image. Information and image (river) are coupled, but the complexity of shared terror is borne to a marked degree through the turns of these anxious line breaks. The closing lines of the poem again shock at the harsh turnabout at each line break:

he goes, [. . .] tunneling past
death sacked into a blind corner,
loving the weight of the shotgun
that will someday dig his grave.

Line Use in a Complete Poem

It is time to discuss line in a complete poem. Although attention is chiefly to line, we will introduce a few topics which are yet to be defined and explained.

"Stepping Westward" was written by British-born American poet Denise Levertov. We will listen for the way she uses line and pause to create tone, tempo, rhythm, and meaning. But as we hear her lines move stanza by stanza, we will consider too her use of the couplet. The subject of "stanza" will be taken up at the end of this chapter.

Stepping Westward

What is green in me
darkens, muscadine.

If woman is inconstant,
good, I am faithful to

ebb and flow, I fall
in season and now

is a time of ripening.
If her part

is to be true,
a north star,

good, I hold steady
in the black sky

and vanish by day,
yet burn there

in blue or above
quilts of cloud.

There is no savor
more sweet, more salt

than to be glad to be
what, woman,

and who, myself,
I am, a shadow

that grows longer as the sun
moves, drawn out

on a thread of wonder.
If I bear burdens

they begin to be remembered
as gifts, goods, a basket

of bread that hurts
my shoulders but closes me

in fragrance. I can
eat as I go.

Through the first line our voice remains expectantly high, then drops at "darkens," and pauses (comma) before the mysterious polysyllable "muscadine," whose rising sound seems to challenge the notion that "darkens" is bad: it may mean deepening, ripening like grapes. The next couplet affirms that conviction by placing "good," in a satisfyingly emphatic position (pause before and after). Had she said, "It is good that woman is inconstant," the idea would be similar but she would lose her voice's emphasis and pride. After the first stanza, the couplets enjamb consistently, creating tension, flow, and continual contrast. If we expect the cliché "in season and out" in the third stanza, "now" surprises us, changing the thought, canceling the cliché, sending us into the next stanza which breaks completely in the middle, another surprise, and drives through to stanza six to "good" again emphasized by coming after a line and stanza break. She both negates the clichés and accepts the contrariness they hint at. The following stanzas develop the paradox of "steady," "vanish," and "burn."

A beautiful passage opens stanza nine: "There is no savor / more sweet, more salt"—perhaps a change from the expected sweet–sour. If our voice suspends in anticipation after "than to be glad to be," it is caught off guard by "what" followed by a comma. Our expectations are again challenged so we must watch punctuation and line break to hear the speaker's flow of sense and tone. Fresh emphasis comes at "a woman," and then line-and-stanza break before "and who, myself" continues the syntactic progress. But with "I am" the syntax again has something else in mind than we perhaps expect. The poem has played with contraries of in–constant, ebb–flow, in–out, day–night, sweet–salt. If that is what woman is, the speaker urges, well then, Great, I'm it! The what–who passage suggests a delight in being itself, lifting the context to metaphysical dimensions, reveling in mysterious wonder. In multiple ways the speaker shows her pleasure in her paradoxical nature and in the contradictions of woman which make her complete, strong, and proud: "I can / eat as I go."

Now the question of the couplets. Couplet suggests unity, two lines that rhyme and often, in traditional couplet verse, end-stop. A couplet makes an explicit argument that one plus one equals a completed statement. "Stepping Westward" is one in a set of ten poems called "Abel's Bride." The speaker (not Biblical but the poet's invention) is ruminating on the nature of her bridehood. Since she sees both a paradox within herself about woman's complexity and a truth about unity in herself, she needs both the couplet unity (also the marriage state) and the irresolution of couplets that are neither completed nor end-stopped. The vocal expression of her speech creates the experiential tone of the whole; we hear in her voice the pairing of each couplet and the movement onward through each. It is her seizing upon those contradictions which define her as woman, and give her joy and pride as she resolves the tensions.

Not only does Levertov write poems with acute attention to the line, but she has carefully thought through what line and line break mean in her verse. In modern poetry more than in traditional poetry, she writes, the line

> incorporates and reveals the *process* of thinking/feeling,
> feeling/thinking, rather than focusing more exclusively on
> its *results*. . . . The most obvious function of the linebreak is
> rhythmic: it can record the slight (but meaningful) hesitations
> between word and word that are characteristic of the mind's
> dance among perceptions but which are not noted by gram-
> matical punctuation. [4]

Syntax with its punctuation is the rational, grammatical structure by which we express thoughts and observations. But our minds are occupied with other things simultaneous with the rational which also need modes of expression. We know that we do not necessarily think in linear progression; nor do we always compose and write in orderly fashion, though standard written expression prescribes a degree of this. So if the mind or emotion is wondering, searching, hesitating, how does grammar express these? Line-break comes into play to record the "mind's dance" through uncertainty, the "hesitations" of the search. Levertov goes on:

> The linebreak is a form of punctuation *additional* to the punc-
> tuation that forms part of the logic of completed thoughts.
> Linebreaks—together with intelligent uses of indentation,
> and other devices for scoring—represent a peculiarly *poetic,*
> alogical, parallel (not competitive) punctuation.

She distinguishes between logical/rational thought and the "alogical,"
what the poet wishes to express which is not counter to logic but simultane-
ous and different. (Elsewhere she says a line-end pause is "equal to half a
comma," but pauses between stanzas are "much harder to evaluate."[5]) We
will later take up indentation as a form of line break.

In "The Idea of Ancestry," Etheridge Knight's voice is personal, conver-
sational, candid in his thoughts about how I, here in a prison cell, fit with
them out there, my wide family.

> 1
>
> Taped to the wall of my cell are 47 pictures: 47 black
> faces: my father, mother, grandmothers (1 dead), grand-
> fathers (both dead), brothers, sisters, uncles, aunts,
> cousins (1st & 2nd), nieces, and nephews. They stare
> across the space at me sprawling on my bunk. I know
> their dark eyes, they know mine. I know their style,
> they know mine. I am all of them, they are all of me;
> they are farmers, I am a thief, I am me, they are thee.

Through this opening stanza's enumeration of family members, Knight's
long lines literally make space. As "They stare / across the space at me," one
feels the distance across his cell—the turn literally moving from one wall
to its opposite—and his distance from them. But as the lines move down,
phrase after phrase, he draws the family together, "I" drawn closer to "them"
inside the line, even though both remain physically apart.

In the first stanza of "Circling the Daughter," Knight controls speech
patterns by many end-stopped lines: the slash in line one is his device to
add a pause of separation that also enforces meaning.

> You came / to be / in the Month of Malcolm,
> And the rain fell with a fierce gentleness,
> Like a martyr's tears,

On the streets of Manhattan when your light was lit;
And the City sang you Welcome. Now I sit,
Trembling in your presence. Fourteen years
Have brought the moon-blood, the roundness,
The girl-giggles, the grand-leaps.
We are touch-tender in our fears.

You break my eyes with your beauty:
Ooouu-oo-baby-I-love-you.

The opening four lines end-stop, the fifth ending in midline, preparing for the I-speaker to begin reflecting. This poem is not about physical space, but about pondering the uncertainties of father–daughter relationships in U.S. history. It is gradual in tempo, sorrowful (Malcolm's death), hesitant in his fatherhood ("Trembling in your presence"), celebrative; then it easily breaks into a sung song, crooned in the italicized stanza.

The Irish poet Eavan Boland says that her line breaks are more like those of the standard Western lyric: they do not illustrate a thought process but establish a mood and emotion. "This Moment" is a remarkably full poem, the brevity of whose lines creates mood by deliberate incompleteness of thought:

A neighborhood.
At dusk.

Things are getting ready
to happen
out of sight.

Stars and moths.
And rinds slanting around fruit.

But not yet.

One tree is black.
One window is yellow as butter.

A woman leans down to catch a child
who has run into her arms
this moment.

Stars rise.
Moths flutter.
Apples sweeten in the dark.

The opening words leave so little said—the speaker's voice stops at each line, and drops, not as if to end a sentence but to create silences, as of the woman listening. In stanza two the lines nervously cite a danger, glancing around with fear. Even her two lines of observation, "stars and moths," are fragments. The middle stanza ventures even less: "But not yet," as if she is scarcely able to look out or assert anything concrete about what she sees. Then come two actual statements, one dark-threatening, the other possibly warm (a home?). And finally the sudden rush of three separate sentences: the child is back, safe, and life can begin moving once more.

To return to Levertov: a line break, she writes, "subtly interrupts a sentence" or "subtly interrupts a phrase or clause."

Boland's poem too utilizes this interruptive power of line to record the mind working through thoughts and emotions.

Line and Vocal Rhythm

If a poem is based on conversational tones and rhythms, even more than the ones seen so far, the speaker's vocal expression—and our voices too as we speak the poem—may require closer attention to sound and emphasis to hear the sense. Here are two poems by Lucille Clifton. Intellectualize them and they roll over and play dead. Speak them and the tone will jump out.

good times

my daddy has paid the rent
and the insurance man is gone
and the lights is back on
and my uncle brud has hit
for one dollar straight
and they is good times
good times
good times

my mamma has made bread
and grampaw has come
and everybody is drunk
and dancing in the kitchen
and singing in the kitchen
oh these is good times

good times
good times

oh children think about the
good times

homage to my hips

these hips are big hips.
they need space to
move around in.
they don't fit into little
petty places. these hips
are free hips.
they don't like to be held back.
these hips have never been enslaved,
they go where they want to go
they do what they want to do.
these hips are mighty hips.
these hips are magic hips.
i have known them
to put a spell on a man and
spin him like a top!

In "good times," Clifton works without the safety net of punctuation. But that is not a difficulty. Her art guides our voice precisely. This poem begins with three complete assertions, until four moves easily into five, and we begin the delightful refrain-repetition.

Ordinarily a repeated line calls for change of vocal emphasis. When William Blake ended his song, "Little Lamb, God bless thee, / Little Lamb, God bless thee" repetition rings out new meanings: else why repeat? So too here. These are good times. Good times. Good times. Repetition normally prompts us to slow down for richer meanings. The final repetition insists on the same: "Oh children, think about the / good times." If we had any doubt that these are really good times, the repetitions assure us of the celebration.

Clifton's "homage to my hips" quickly enjambs: "they need space to / move around in." Reading the lines straight through cancels the stress on "move," the verbal imbalance of a broken infinitive, and the bodily shift that accompanies the word. After several end-stopped lines—"these hips have never been enslaved"—she readies the final, decisive physical movement:

> i have known them
> to put a spell on a man and
> spin him like a top!

Only with that pause can she hit "spin" with such delicious meaning, fun, and confidence. The poem is about her physicality and the real physicality of its recitation: the lines make one move.

Poems ordinarily address specific emotional experiences. Since emotional confusion, which unfortunately may not be uncommon, can stimulate anger, depression, sickness—none of them healthy feelings to store in our bodies—we need to understand our emotions. So we strive to describe and express their precise nature. If poems express a wide range of emotions, as wide as our human emotional range itself, we need to consider how poems can carve subtle emotional distinctions out of the welter of confusingly mixed ones.

One day in class we were looking at Robert Hass's "Heroic Simile" (quoted and discussed under "Simile," chapter six) and a student had written on the board from his essay: "A dying hero gives off a stillness to the air." The students were frustrated at finding a way into its tone. Suddenly one of them erupted: "That's misquoted! The line should read

> A hero, dying,
> gives off stillness to the air."

Without question, this was one of the best mistakes of the semester. The error illustrated almost everything essential about line break and word position. The placement of "dying," its declining sound ("*dy*-ing") repeating that of "*he*-ro," set off with commas, the silence after it, the almost soundless second line emphasizing "stillness," revealed the true tone beautifully. There could be no doubt of the exact sense of loss and longing contained in those lines.

But even as we say "loss and longing" we know that such words do not cover the complexity of emotion the lines themselves reveal. What does "hero" mean, to us, to anyone? And a dying one? If the air is still, what is it that we feel, what is missing? As we hear the movement of the lines, and the disconcerting drop at line break, we become able to speak the lines and

feel the distinct emotions expressed through these words. Our point here
is multiple: words do mean. The poem's own words create and character-
ize precisely the emotion(s) which cannot be captured in alternate words.
While line is a crucial instrument of this effect, other prosodic elements
(such as meter) also have a bearing. One useful (though admittedly strange)
way of hearing the impact of line and sound in verse is to make a conscious
mistake: change a word or two, rewrite a few lines, or even paraphrase the
poem (turning it into prose, which eliminates sound, tempo, rhythm, and
other elements of verse).

Here is a set of similar-looking lines that express different emotions.
First from Charles Olson's "Maximus, to Himself":

> I have had to learn the simplest things
> last. Which made for difficulties.

What Olson is saying is obvious enough: "I'm a slow learner and that's
caused trouble." But how does he *feel* about that fact? The tempo of the first
line is methodical, unbroken, the pitch rising slightly on "simplest things,"
preparing for the abrupt drop to "last." The separate dependent clause that
completes the line contributes a sober but not depressing comment.

In the opening of John Logan's "Three Moves," we again find the end
of the sentence placed in line two:

> Three moves in six months and I remain
> the same.

This is the same kind of line break. But is his emotion the same as Olson's?
Reserving further examination for a moment, line break is used to create
meaning through a distinct kind of pause and emphasis.

A third example of this kind of line break, this time from Gerard Manly
Hopkins' "Wreck of the Deutschland":

> Thou mastering me
> God! giver of breath and bread.

Hopkins does not begin with a statement like "I have had to learn . . . ," but
with an exclamatory phrase. Yet the completion of the phrase, "God" on
the second line, is similar in structure to Olson's and Logan's second lines.
We continue the second line to complete the statement. If we knew that
this poem was about the wreck of a ship called the *Deutschland* in which

a group of nuns were drowned and that Hopkins, a Catholic priest, was concerned how to remember their tragic deaths, would we hear the lines differently? Or is the speaker's emotional tone complete within these lines? More dramatic than in the prior poems, Hopkins's placement of "God" is daring because it risks misreading as exasperated with "God," or sick of being mastered. If our principle is right, we can rely upon line to tell us to be exactly sure what each poem means.

For the sake of contributing to the discussion, we will add a few thoughts on Hopkins, Logan, and Olson. With the Hopkins poem, the word sounds of "mastering me" hold high, accepting the paradox of willing to be mastered; then at line break accepting "God!" there is a rest in faith, a rest confirmed in God as a *giver* of both spirit and body. Were we to exchange "bread and breath," the sound and sense would convey a different acceptance—if any. The tempo of Logan's first line is unhurried, for there is a kind of pulse by which we stress each word group not by pausing but by slight elongation: "Three moves // in six months // and I remain," that prepares for a fall of spirit after "remain," unlike Olson's line break that throws emphasis on "last." Olson's emotion is not as devastating as Logan's; rather, his irritation is tempered with matter-of-factness in the steady tempo of line one. In each case, the structure of the line allows us to hear the exact emotional state of each speaker.

Extending the Line Further

It should not be assumed that every poet would subscribe to the principles of line we have laid out here. Like any artists, poets need to explore ways of extending their craft, their meanings, which may be accomplished by manipulating the line in new ways. To illustrate, we need look no further than the work of the same Gerard Manly Hopkins. Normally, English verse is composed of feet of two or three syllables, iamb, dactyl, and so on (terms to be examined under "Meter"). Hopkins's idea of "sprung rhythm" "is measured by feet of from one to four syllables." For special effects "any number of weak or slack syllables may be used." He also distinguished *running rhythm* which puts stress on the second syllable of a foot, unstress–stress, from *falling* in which the second syllable is unstressed, stress–unstress.[6] In order to achieve his measure of stress he might vary the syllables of lines and, more to the point, run through line breaks to finish the foot in the next line. Here is "No Worst":

> No worst, there is none. Pitched past pitch of grief,
> More pangs will, schooled at forepangs, wilder wring.
> Comforter, where, where is your comforting?
> Mary, mother of us, where is your relief?
> My cries heave, herds-long, huddle in a main, a chief-
> Woe, wórld-sorrow; on an áge-old anvil wince and sing—
> Then lull, then leave off. Fury had shrieked 'No ling-
> Ering! Let me be fell: force I must be brief.'
> O the mind, mind has mountains; cliffs of fall
> Frightful, sheer, not man's fathoming. Hold them cheap
>   no-man-fathomed.
> May who ne'er hung there. Nor does long our small
> Durance deal with that steep or deep. Here! creep,
> Wretch, under a comfort serves in a whirlwind: all
> Life death does end and each day dies with sleep.

Line five ends with a stress "chief-"; "Woe" on the next line completes the falling foot. More dramatically, "No ling- / Ering!" radically enjambs a half-word onto the next line. In other poems Hopkins makes it perfectly clear there is to be no pause at line ends. For example, in "To Seem the Stranger" the first lines run:

> To seem the stranger lies my lot, my life
> Among strangers. Father and mother dear,
> Brothers and sisters are in Christ not near
> And he my peace / my parting, sword and strife.
> England, whose honour O all my heart woos, wife
> To my creating thought, would neither hear
> Me, were I pleading, plead nor do I: I wear-
> Y of idle a being but by where wars are rife. . . .

Whereas the first line's "life / Among" seems a normal line break, "wear- / **Y**" is far more strongly enjambed. The word break exposes the rhyme word—dear–near, hear–wear—but the voice moves on toward new meaning with "**Y**." Hopkins is obviously driving his lines to achieve more than he believes is possible with line-break pauses, and given the amazing power of his verse, one is quite happy to agree.

Stanza

If the line is a unit, often a unit of meaning, at the end of which there is a turn, a *stanza* is a group of lines usually set off on the page by space, indentation, number, or set rhyme scheme (ABBA), some visible device to mark a discrete group of lines. Stanzas can be of uniform size, such as two lines or four lines, with or without rhyme. Many of our principles about line are equally applicable to *stanza*. That is, there is often a turn or pause at stanza end; enjambment of stanzas (the sentence runs from one stanza into the next) is usually significant; so are changes in the number of lines, in rhyme scheme, line length, and the like. In short, a stanza shapes meaning as line does, and just as lines move forward and down, so do stanzas.

In defining line, it was mentioned that in staged Greek verse, the movement of the line and of the dance often coincided, with a pause at the end. Stanza, too, is allied with dance.[7] The ode, which means song, is a poem often associated with its earliest great practitioner, Pindar. It is a form divided into three stanzas called *strophes*, meaning a turn, as in a choral dance on stage: the *strophe* (move) is followed by the *antistrophe* (return) and ends with the *epode* (stand or end).

Just as lines move and end at certain places, so a stanza may be complete in itself as a syntactic unit, and it may use rhyme to accentuate completion. A sentence can also move through a stanza or a number of stanzas, developing a long arc of relationship and continuity between units. While there are potentially as many kinds of stanzaic form as there are poems, what matters is that we identify the structural unit of the stanza and that we recognize the expressive function of the stanza in the speaker's words. That is, not only *what* it is itself—its length and shape—but *how* it stands in relation to what comes before and what follows, how a stanza moves across and down into the next stanza and stanzas.

Whereas in traditional verse the number of lines in a stanza is often determined by the genre, such as a ballad's four-line stanza (ABCB), stanza size can vary according to the needs of the poem, as we saw in Herbert's "The Church-floor." In Edmund Waller's "Go, Lovely Rose," lines vary four,

eight, four, eight, eight syllables. Changed indentation also suggests varia-
tion in tone.

> Go, lovely, rose—
> Tell her that wastes her time and me
> That now she knows,
> When I resemble her to thee,
> How sweet and fair she seems to be.

In twentieth-century and contemporary verse, stanza size is often deter-
mined by the nature of the speaker's expression. Boland's stanza form in
"This Moment" is determined by the speaker, a taut wariness of the violence
she senses lurking. In "good times," Clifton's two stanzas narrate the world
of the family, linking first to second by three identical refrain lines: "oh these
is good times / good times / good times," and concluding the whole with a
summary pair of lines: "oh children think about the / good times." In both
poems the stanza is set off by space, but the function of each is unique to
its individual expression.

William Carlos Williams's "To a Poor Old Woman" has four stanzas of
four lines (the title is included in the first).

> *To a Poor Old Woman*
>
> munching a plum on
> the street a paper bag
> of them in her hand
>
> They taste good to her
> They taste good
> to her. They taste
> good to her
>
> You can see it by
> the way she gives herself
> to the one half
> sucked out in her hand
>
> Comforted
> a solace of ripe plums
> seeming to fill the air
> They taste good to her

The integrity of the first stanza is his seeing her, in a place, acting; the second reveals her reaction to the plums. In the third, his attention turns to her actions, and is delicately enjambed to her consolation in those luscious plums. Each stanza has its distinct function and its link to the rest.

In both line and stanza, pause is measured by *duration*: how long we pause; and by *quality*: how we vocally express the nature of the pause or hesitation (such as with doubt, expectation, sorrow). We hear and speak line breaks and stanza breaks slightly differently. If a stanza closes syntactically, the pause can be as long as the duration of a period or longer to accommodate the stanza's finality and the space before the next stanza. If a stanza enjambs to the next, the duration and the quality of pause will depend on context (of which more below). In the Levertov poem:

> What is green in me
> darkens, muscadine.
>
> If woman is inconstant,
> good, I am faithful to
>
> ebb and flow, I fall
> in season and now
>
> is a time of ripening.
> If her part

The voice drops at "darkens," pauses, and stops at "muscadine": end of line, sentence, stanza. The pause at "faithful to" has a possibly similar *duration*, but the voice quality registers incompleteness before the example of faithful inconstancy in "ebb and flow." Because the voice rises at "and now" to end the next stanza, our pause may be a more dramatic silence of expectation.

In a word, no one factor determines length or quality of the silence. In another word: the movement across each line pauses at the turn of the verse with a kind of downward draw through the poem: across, through, down. Interruptions and/or accelerations in this movement across and down are often achieved by line and stanza.

Marking Stanzas

The various devices for marking separate stanzas indicate different relationships among stanzas. Numbered stanzas usually indicate a major division. Here Robert Francis tells of "The Swimmer":

I

Observe how he negotiates his way
With trust and the least violence, making
The stranger friend, the enemy ally.
The depth that could destroy gently supports him.
With water he defends himself from water.
Danger he leans on, rests in. The drowning sea
Is all he has between himself and drowning.

II

What lover ever lay more mutually
With his beloved, his always-reaching arms
Stroking in smooth and powerful caresses?
Some drown in love as in dark water, and some
By love are strongly held as the green sea
Now holds the swimmer. Indolently he turns
To float.—The swimmer floats, the lover sleeps.

Once we have the image of the swimmer's action, stanza two expands the figure. Not that it is hard to catch the connection, but the numbered separation allows development of each element of the comparison, as stanza comments on stanza. The silence is crystal clear as we await a transition to applied figure, the turn of each line ("always-reaching arms") held just long enough to hear the click of connecting metaphor.

Obviously, the principle of visible breaks may not always hold. We may wonder whether the breaks in the following poem by Denise Levertov are actual stanza breaks or some other form of division.

That Day

Across a lake in Switzerland, fifty years ago,
light was jousting with long lances, fencing with broadswords
back and forth among cloudy peaks and foothills.
We watched from a small pavilion, my mother and I,
enthralled.
             And then, behold, a shaft, a column,

> a defined body, not of light but of silver rain,
> formed and set out from the distant shore, leaving behind
> the silent feints and thrusts, and advanced
> unswervingly, at a steady pace,
> toward us.
>
>   I knew this! I'd seen it! Not the sensation
> of déjà vu: it was Blake's inkwash vision,
> 'The Spirit of God Moving Upon the Face of the Waters'!
> The column steadily came on
> across the lake toward us; on each side of it,
> there was no rain. We rose to our feet, breathless—
> and then it reached us, took us
> into its veil of silver, wrapped us
> in finest weave of wet,
> and we laughed for joy, astonished.

Whatever we call these breaks, their visible indentations coincide with a change of the speaker's perception. She is at first a relaxed, vacationing observer: she and her mother are safely seated, and the play of natural light is entirely satisfactory to them. But the single word "enthralled" ends the section abruptly, followed by line and "stanza" break. Indentation begins the next section: "And then, behold, . . . " they see an actual "body." Whatever we call this break, we know something has changed in her condition and observation, more than just her "sensation."

Again at the short line "toward us" we are stopped. Indentation prepares for the voice change to exclamation, recognition, and intensely conscious observation: "The column steadily came on / across the lake toward us; on each side of it, / there was no rain." The lines shorten, the tempo slows and attention alerts to the inexorable advance. The final five line-end words reveal in miniature her experience: *breathless, took us, wrapped us, wet, astonished.*

What this stanza form does is separate the stages of her experience; distinguish each level of her consciousness; reveal through line- and stanza-break the movement of the out-there to the in-here; and shift the tone from tourist-in-nature to visionary, an internalizing of that "wet" "inkwash" into bone-deep joy. And these stanza-like breaks do more: they create the experience of vision. As is true of many of Levertov's (and others') poems, inside the spoken movement of these stanzas resides the meaning of the poem. The pauses are made purposefully, each stanza a segment of experience, the downward flow of stanzas creating the complete event. Allowing this poem to lead us through the speaker's experience replicates her experience into "a defining body."

For a different example of the way stanzas may function, we look at "Adam's Curse" by William Butler Yeats. Somewhat like Levertov, Yeats links stanza one to two by breaking a line after six syllables and indenting the four syllables of the next (like a ten-syllable line).

Adam's Curse

We sat together at one summer's end,
That beautiful mild woman, your close friend,
And you and I, and talked of poetry.
I said: "A line will take us hours maybe;
Yet if it does not seem a moment's thought,
Our stitching and unstitching has been naught.
Better go down upon your marrow-bones
And scrub a kitchen pavement, or break stones
Like an old pauper, in all kinds of weather;
For to articulate sweet sounds together
Is to work harder than all these, and yet
Be thought an idler by the noisy set
Of bankers, schoolmasters, and clergymen
The martyrs call the world."

                      And thereupon
That beautiful mild woman for whose sake
There's many a one shall find out all heartache
On finding that her voice is sweet and low
Replied: "To be born woman is to know—
Although they do not talk of it at school—
That we must labour to be beautiful."

I said: "It's certain there is no fine thing
Since Adam's fall but needs much labouring.
There have been lovers who thought love should be

So much compounded of high courtesy
That they would sigh and quote with learned looks
Precedents out of beautiful old books;
Yet now it seems an idle trade enough."

We sat grown quiet at the name of love;
We saw the last embers of daylight die,
And in the trembling blue-green of the sky
A moon, worn as if it had been a shell
Washed by time's waters as they rose and fell
About the stars and broke in days and years.

I had a thought for no one's but your ears:
That you were beautiful, and that I strove
To love you in the old high way of love;
That it had all seemed happy, and yet we'd grown
As weary-hearted as that hollow moon.

Whereas the shortened last line (six syllables rather than ten) of the first stanza of fourteen lines adds a feeling of irresolution and "curse," the last three stanzas are linked by rhyme as if not quite separated (all stanzas are end-stopped): "enough" and "love," "years" and "ears." Each stanza introduces a different speaker or topic as if each stanza is complete, yet the stanzas are uneven in length (14, 7, 7, 6, 5 lines) like broken connections. The connecting and separating of stanzas declare that the curse (part of which is poetry making itself) is complex and not resolved by talking, even for "hours maybe."

Notes

1. T. B. L. Webster (*The Greek Chorus*, London: Methuen & Co Ltd, 1970) illustrates thoroughly the dancers' pause at the end of lines of verse: "The hexameter is a long line with a well-marked pause at the end, and would be sung 'walking.'" There is also "a short line with pause at the end, an admirable 'striding' line which could be used either for marching or dancing." (54–55; cf: "Literary Sources" to ca. p. 87 on Pindar.) See also M. L. West, *Ancient Greek Music* (Oxford: Clarendon Press, 1992), 153 ff.

2. Northrop Frye, *The Great Code* (New York: Harcourt Brace Jovanovich, 1981), 8.

3. Northrop Frye, *Anatomy of Criticism* (Princeton, NJ: Princeton University Press, 1957), 263 f.

4. Denise Levertov, "On the Function of the Line," in *New & Selected Essays*, (New York: A New Directions Book, 1992), 79.

5. Denise Levertov, "Line Breaks, Stanza-Spaces, and the Inner Voice," in *Essays*, p. 90.

6. "Author Preface," Norman H. Mackenzie., ed., introduction to *The Poetical Works of Gerard Manley Hopkins* (Oxford: Clarendon Press, 1990), 115–116.

7. William Mullen, *Choreia: Pindar and Dance* (Princeton: Princeton University Press, 1982), 90 ff. See also Lillian B. Lawler, *The Dance of the Ancient Greek Theatre* (Iowa City: University of Iowa Press, 1964), 11 ff.

Chapter Two

Sound

What does it mean to say that there is *sound* in poetry? Does poetry *have* sound or *is* it sound? For instance, sounds are *described* in the line "The curfew tolls the knell of parting day," and in "the tintinnabulation of the bells, bells, bells." We usually identify sound effects by devices like a*ssonance*, repeated vowel sounds; *alliteration*, repeated consonant sounds; *onomatopoeia*, meaning contained in the sound, like "Whack," "Buzz"; or sound links between words, as in Tennyson's "The Lady of Shalott":

> On <u>ei</u>ther <u>side</u> the river <u>lie</u>
> Long **fie**lds of barl**ey** and of <u>rye,</u>

It is, however, the sound of all words in poetry that concern us. The sound of a word itself expresses *meaning and emotion*. Musical sounds may be described in "tolls" and "knell" but we can also speak of the sound of the expression "parting day." Word choices convey far more meaning and emotion than their denotation. Even in our everyday speech we know the difference between the sounds of "Shhh" and "Shut up."

In chapter one we quoted Robert Francis's "The Sound I Listened For" for the way it describes the movement of line. We can listen to it again for its use of word sounds:

> What I remember is the ebb and flow of sound

That summer morning as the mower came and went
And came again, crescendo and diminuendo,
And always when the sound was loudest how it ceased
A moment while he backed the horses for the turn,
The rapid clatter giving place to the slow click
And the mower's voice. That was the sound I listened for.

Quiet summer-morning word sounds (for example, repeated "m" and "o") fill the opening lines; even the slightly harder consonants of "crescendo and diminuendo" are quieted by the polysyllables. But the consonants become more noisy: "he backed the horses for the turn, / The rapid clatter . . . ," then become quiet "giving place to the slow click / And the mower's voice." In short, the sounds of the poem imitate the meaning of the words themselves, and we too listen for the poet-mower's sounds.

This is A. E. Housman's poem XXXV from *A Shropshire Lad*:

On the idle hill of summer,
   Sleepy with the flow of streams,
Far I hear the steady drummer
   Drumming like a noise in dreams.

In this beautiful picture of an idle hill, summer, sleepy flow of streams, the words' meanings harmonize with their mild vowels and consonants. Yet already in "steady drummer" the consonants grow stronger and continue to do so in the disturbing "Drumming . . . noise . . . dream." The poem goes on:

Far and near and low and louder
   On the roads of earth go by
Dear to friends and food for powder,
   Soldiers marching, all to die.

East and west on fields forgotten
   Bleach the bones of comrades slain,
Lovely lads and dead and rotten;
   None that go return again.

Far the calling bugles hollo,
   High the screaming fife replies,
Gay the files of scarlet follow
   Woman bore me, I will rise.

The ominous tone is not in the words' denotations (until the end) but in the recurring rumbling "-r" and low vowels: far, near, low, louder. Before the poem does, the sounds tell us we are hearing about war and death.

When composing "Anthem for a Doomed Youth," Wilfred Owen originally wrote, "What minute bells for those who die so fast." Upon the advice of fellow poet Siegfried Sassoon, he revised the lines to:

> What passing-bells for these who die as cattle?
> > Only the monstrous anger of the guns.
> > Only the stuttering rifles' rapid rattle
> Can patter out their hasty orisons.

The image is changed to animals and the sound is also changed: the hard, painful consonants in "cattle" are repeated in "stuttering," "rattle" and "patter" like staccato gun fire.

> No mockeries now for them; no prayers nor bells,
> > Nor any voice of mourning save the choirs,—
> The shrill, demented choirs of wailing shells;
> > And bugles calling for them from sad shires.
>
> What candles may be held to speed them all?
> > Not in the hands of boys but in their eyes
> Shall shine the holy glimmers of good-byes.
> > The pallor of girls' brows shall be their pall;
> Their flowers the tenderness of patient minds,
> And each slow dusk a drawing-down of blinds.

Uses of Sound in Two Poems

To hear how the sound of words functions in complete poems, we select two by Stanley Kunitz, the first based on the suicide of his father before Stanley was born, the second on a seasonal transition in nature.

The Portrait

> My mother never forgave my father
> for killing himself,
> especially at such an awkward time

and in a public park,
that spring
when I was waiting to be born.
She locked his name
in her deepest cabinet
and would not let him out,
though I could hear him thumping.
When I came down from the attic
with the pastel portrait in my hand
of a long-lipped stranger
with a brave moustache
and deep brown level eyes,
she ripped it into shreds
without a single word
and slapped me hard.
In my sixty-fourth year
I can feel my cheek
still burning.

As we read this poem aloud, we listen for the sounds of the lines, the way they move and change. For example, when the "v" of "never" is repeated, greater weight falls on "forgave," as if the mother's resentment is crucial. The hard consonants of "killing" continue in "awkward time" and "public park." When attention turns to the boy, the sound is quiet: "that spring / when I was waiting to be born." Change of sound means change of meaning and emotion. In lines seven to ten, we hear the mother's actions and feelings in the sharp sounds of "locked," "deepest cabinet," and the determined "-t" sounds of "not let . . . out." Again returning to the boy's feelings, gentler sounds follow at "though I could hear him thumping"—with a noticeably warmer rhythmic pulse.

In the third sentence (to line eighteen) the young boy descends step by step, line by line, eyeing each detail of the portrait, until he is stopped by the violent "ripped it into shreds." At the end, the speaker places "still" not as "still feel" but as "still burning" so its consonant and vowel sound will echo "feel" and intensify the final word. In the word selection we hear the speaker's emotion progressing, not only growing up but reflecting precisely on the complicated tensions of his experiences.

We will return to "The Portrait," but take up now the second poem by Kunitz:

End of Summer

An agitation of the air,
A perturbation of the light
Admonished me the unloved year
Would turn on its hinge that night.

I stood in the disenchanted field
Amid the stubble and the stones,
Amazed, while a small worm lisped to me
The song of my marrow-bones.

Blue poured into summer blue,
A hawk broke from his cloudless tower,
The roof of the silo blazed, and I knew
That part of my life was over.

Already the iron door of the north
Clangs open: birds, leaves, snows
Order their populations forth,
And a cruel wind blows.

The sounds of "agitation" and "perturbation" first create tone. If we are unsure what sort of disturbance he felt, those polysyllables suggest a particular disturbance that is sufficient for us. (In an interview, Kunitz said that the perturbation he witnessed was the beating wings of a flight of geese.) We listen for indications of change in the sound. The speaker's emotional uncertainty lies in his consonants: "I stood in the disenchanted field / Amid the stubble and the stones"; but the sound of "Amazed . . . small worm lisped" tells he stopped to listen to something internal. At the grating sound of "hinge" he knows hard things will follow. And certainly the final lines— "iron door . . . north / Clangs open," "a cruel wind blows"—say everything now is going to be difficult.

In these two poems sharp or soft sounds vary according to context; neither the same consonants nor the same vowels have the same meaning. The importance and meaning of sounds depend on the word in which they appear; on their placement in lines (Kunitz's strong suit); on the words associated and contrasted in sound and in meaning; and on the sense of the sentence(s) and stanza(s).

To go back to "The Portrait," we may notice a surprising number of "p" sounds: "public park," "spring," "thumping," "pastel portrait," "ripped," "slapped," and so forth. The first, "public park," is emphatic because of its place at end of the line, the sharp consonants that end each word, and the emotional content: the locale shames the mother. With "deepest" the "p," along with adjacent consonants, continues to be insistent, but it mellows in "thumping" for focus has moved to the boy. In each case the sound impact of the "p" is different, sometimes emphatic, sometimes almost lost, as in "lipped."

Let us clarify: we do not hold that meaning attaches to an individual letter. Rather, the sound of a letter has meaning. Does the letter "l" have meaning? No. The poet Thomas Gray said he could not delete a certain word "for it begins with the letter l." To Gray the "l" did not have special meaning, but it was a most pleasing sound he hated to lose. Alfred Lord Tennyson warned against frequent use of "s" because it would become intrusive and unpleasant. The issue was not what "s" meant, but rather that excessive sibilance would become distracting.

What Vowels and Consonants Sound Like

One of the things we learned while teaching poetry classes is that the deeper we moved into a particular poem, the greater was the need for language to describe what we were hearing and to enable us to speak a poem effectively and truthfully. Since hearing and speaking poetry is so much our concern, we felt we had to know more about sound itself, about vowels and consonants, so we could identify what we were hearing and saying. Distinctions made by phonetics (the discipline that describes sounds by their generation within the throat and mouth) were extremely valuable in our examination of sound. That is, hearing sound differences is not a matter of whimsy, of my opinion over yours. If we wish to move further into any poem to hear it well, detailed information becomes necessary.[1]

Letters are either vowels or consonants. Vowels are usually called *long* or *short*—long being the sounds of the letter itself: "a" as in "day." Short is a term for everything that does not say the name of the letter: "a" in "that." Neither *long* nor *short* is an exact description.[2] A more pertinent factor is that vowels can be elongated, lengthened so that their sound becomes more emphatic. In "The Portrait" we elongate "deep brown . . . eyes" to reflect his sense of wonderment. In "End of Summer" when we say "The roof . . . blazed, and I knew," noun and verbs are elongated, unlike the terse "hawk broke."

While consonants ordinarily sound like themselves, a "d" like a "d," an "r" like an "r," consonants do change sound in relation to adjacent consonants and vowels: "th" in "that" and "mouth" sound different. Consonants may also be elongated, as in "blazed" and "hinge" above. Compare the different use of "blow," first from John Donne's *Holy Sonnets,* number seven, the second made-up:

> a) At the round earth's imagined corners, *blow*
>   Your trumpets, Angels.

> b) Slowly *blow* out the flame.

Some poets make a point to exploit the effects of consonants. One of the more notable, certainly, is Wallace Stevens in, for example, "A High-Toned Old Christian Woman":

> Poetry is the supreme fiction, madame.
> Take the moral law and make a nave of it
> And from the nave build haunted heaven. Thus,
> The conscience is converted into palms,
> Like windy citherns hankering for hymns.
> We agree in principle. That's clear. But take
> The opposing law and make a peristyle,
> And from the peristyle project a masque
> Beyond the planets. Thus, our bawdiness,
> Unpurged by epitaph, indulged at last,
> Is equally converted into palms,
> Squiggling like saxophones. And palm for palm,
> Madame, we are where we began. Allow,
> Therefore, that in the planetary scene
> Your disaffected flagellants, well-stuffed,
> Smacking their muzzy bellies in parade,
> Proud of such novelties of the sublime,
> Such tink and tank and tunk-a-tunk-tunk,

> May, merely may, madame, whip from themselves
> A jovial hullabaloo among the spheres.
> This will make widows wince. But fictive things
> Wink as they will. Wink most when widows wince.

We hear Stevens's humorous crashing of consonant upon consonant: "Poetry," "peristyle," "planets," "Unpurged." Or "disaffected flagellants, well-stuffed." The tone from the opening, "Poetry is the supreme fiction, madame," is emphatic (almost, we might wonder, over the top). Some consonants imitate the sound of the thing: "Squiggling like saxophones," or "tink and tank and tunk-a-tunk-tunk." What about that "h": "haunted heaven," "hankering for hymns"? A consonant with little sound itself, the "h" forces exactly that breathy sound of . . . what, breathlessness? Faked passion? Clearly part of the sound movement of the poem, we cannot miss that huffing aspiration. Of course, Stevens also loves vowels: "fictive things / Wink as they will. Wink most when widows wince." Plenty of humor to go around here, not without a bit of mockery!

One way to detect the variations of vowel and consonant sounds is to observe the shape of the mouth as we pronounce them. First consonants. Phonetics distinguishes *voiced* and *voiceless* sounds. A simple sound without any vibration of the throat is voiceless: there is only a hiss as we say the initial "s" in "send." But there is voiced sound in the "z" of "zero."

Now vowels: we open our mouths widely to sound A. Our mouth changes shape as we go to each succeeding vowel: E, I, O, U. Holding a hand against the throat will register the change of location and degree of vibration. The same experiment can demonstrate the range of so-called short vowels: for example, the "i" in "shift," the "e" in "self," the "o" in "box." Reciting a poem is a physical act that involves projecting breath not just from the front of the throat and lips, but drawing breath down to the diaphragm and letting it sound outwards, resonating. We also recognize that the mouth needs a certain amount of time to reshape itself from vowel to vowel—say from O to E—an effort that creates pauses, spaces, and variation in tempo. (Although we here present vowel sounds as if they were pronounced uniformly, *regional variants* and *dialects* in the United States, as in other English speaking countries, change letter and word sounds.)

At this point we can draw some conclusions: Sounds are a natural part of speech and are integral to poetry. Letters do not have inherent meanings;

the sounds of letters have meaning. Vowel sounds can be distinguished by their so-called length; their elongation varies with context and contributes greatly to mood. Consonant sounds vary—hard, soft, sharp, mellow—and can be elongated like vowels. Sound variation is physically discernible.

We return to exploring ways of hearing a poem's sound. Just as we said that line can distinguish subtle changes in emotion, so too can sound, and it is that we examine now.

Here is the opening of Denise Levertov's "Where is the Angel?"

> Where is the angel for me to wrestle?
> No driving snow in the glass bubble,
> but mild September.
>
> Outside, the stark shadows
> menace, and fling their huge arms about
> unheard. I breathe

The sounds of the first lines—"angel," "wrestle," "driving," "glass"—may not seem particularly hard, but against the banality of "mild September" we hear a conflict of images, intensified in the consonants of stanza two, "outside," "stark shadows," "menace." Inside the ball she can only "breathe," scarcely breathing it seems, soundlessly. The poem continues,

> I breathe
> a tepid air, the blur
> of asters, of brown fern and gold-dust
> seems to murmur,

The visual dullness—the asters a blur, the fern dead—parallels her inert life inside the ball. It goes on:

> and that's what I hear, only that.
> Such clear walls of curved glass:
> I see the violent gesticulations
>
> and feel—no, not nothing. But in this
> gentle haze, nothing commensurate.
> It is pleasant in here. History
>
> mouths, volume turned off. A band of iron,
> like they put round a split tree,
> circles my heart. In here

it is pleasant, but when I open
my mouth to speak, I too
am soundless. Where is the angel

to wrestle with me and wound
not my thigh but my throat,
so curses and blessings flow storming out

and the glass shatters, and the iron sunders?

The shift of "to wrestle" from line one to the final stanza here, changes its sound and meaning, for it becomes part of her questioning cry that concludes the poem, with consonants strong with anxious determination. The speaker's perception of her inner life as pleasant but without human life or consequence forces her to reach for the harsher world to stimulate her voice. This poem's sounds warn us not to be fooled into a simple equation: hard is bad, soft is good. (Levertov's angel comes from the Old Testament, the glass ball a snow-glass paperweight.)

In Robert Hass's "Picking Blackberries . . .":

August is dust here. Drought
stuns the road,
but juice gathers in the berries.

the opening lines echo "-gust," "dust," "stuns," the final "t"s accentuating the words. The abrupt sense of overpowering heat would appear destructive. But (not by way of contrast, as in Levertov's) the heat itself causes the gathering juice! The delight in the juiciness lies in the softer consonants—and the low vowels steadily and pleasurably rise: "jUice gAthers In the bErrIEs." It is not accidental that the reader's mouth and tongue change shape while moving from line one to two to three and to the following lines:

We pick them in the hot
Slow-motion of mid morning.

As we have seen how similar sounds change by context, the "t" in "hot" is not like in "dust" but a breathy pause (line break): the work is slow and of deep pleasure—he tells later of his

beard stained purple
by the word *juice*.

The poem is about the luscious sound of words as much as about juicy berries.

Galway Kinnell's "Blackberry Eating" is equally luscious, and the physical activity of pronouncing the words becomes essential to our experience of the poem.

> I love to go out in late September
> among the fat, overripe, icy, black blackberries
> to eat blackberries for breakfast,
> the stalks very prickly, a penalty
> they earn for knowing the black art
> of blackberry making; and as I stand among them
> lifting the stalks to my mouth, the ripest berries
> fall almost unbidden to my tongue,
> as words sometimes do, certain peculiar words
> like *strengths* or *squinched* or *broughamed*
> many-lettered, one-syllabled lumps,
> which I squeeze, squinch open, and splurge well
> in the silent, startled, icy, black language
> of blackberry eating in late September.

One of the best-known poems in the English language is John Milton's *Lycidas*. Since it is an elegy (a poem about someone's death), we anticipate in it an expression of sorrow. Even without knowledge of the classical meanings of certain images or the origin of the name Lycidas, we can hear a great deal of the movement of experiential emotion in the poem. It begins like this:

> Yet once more, O ye laurels, and once more
> Ye myrtles brown, with ivy never sere,
> I come to pluck your berries harsh and crude,
> And with forc'd fingers rude,
> Shatter your leaves before the mellowing year.
> Bitter constraint, and sad occasion dear,
> Compels me to disturb your season due:
> For Lycidas is dead, dead ere his prime,
> Young Lycidas, and hath not left his peer:

The poem's declaration that Lycidas (a pastoral name in place of the actual, Edward King) is dead is no guarantee that the speaker's emotion is sorrow, or only sorrow. At the start the emotion lies in the descending sounds of "Yet once more," repeated; it lies in the darkness of "brown" (image and sound), in the painful "sere" and the consonants of "harsh and crude," "forced fingers rude." That unnerving "eer" sound in "sere" reechoes in "year," "dear," "peer."

Painful emotions do not account for all emotions in *Lycidas*. Yes, sorrow is evident. But do we not also hear violence in harsh–crude–forc'd–shatter–bitter? Can this coexist with sorrow? In lines 37–39 we hear a more profound sorrow, like despair:

> But O the heavy change, now thou art gone,
> Now thou art gone, and never must return!

Or later, when speaking of the mistreatment of the poor faithful (sheep) by corrupt Anglican bishops (pastors) we hear something else:

> their lean and flashy songs
> Grate on their scrannel pipes of wretched straw.
> The hungry sheep look up, and are not fed . . .

This is anger, the hard sounds of rage! And there is yet further emotional movement. Elegy may be about death, but it is also about our human struggle to find solace. And solace for Milton is found in Christian resurrection of the dead.

> Weep no more, woeful shepherds, weep no more,
> For Lycidas your sorrow is not dead,
> Sunk though he be beneath the wat'ry floor,

The speaker's intricate trail of emotion, exactly expressed in the sounds of the poem, has indeed moved to the present condition of consolation where the sounds declare hope:

> So sinks the day-star in the ocean bed,
> And yet anon repairs his drooping head,
> And tricks his beams, and with new-spangled ore,
> Flames in the forehead of the morning sky:

In a word, Lycidas is now in heaven among the saints.

Notes

1 In ordinary usage, vowels are typified as long or short. For example a long vowel is sounded as the letter itself: the "a" in "day"; the "e" of "see"; the "i" of "mind"; the "o" of "no"; the "u" of "use." Other vowel sounds are called short, such as the "a" in "dark" or "stand"; "e" of "text"; "i" of "it" or "first"; "o" of "on" or "log"; "u" of "must." As soon becomes obvious, the term 'short' does not account for the great variety of sounds of, for instance, the letter "a." The "e" at times almost disappears (called a schwa) as does the "e" of "the": "Where is the car?" Vowel sounds vary too in the context of words and other letters.

2 Physically, as we speak, sounds are generated in our throats, and as they pass through our mouths, they may be altered or stopped by lips or teeth or inner parts of the mouth: the alveolar ridge, palate, velum, or uvula. For example, sounds pronounced by the lips are called labials, such as "b," dentals by the teeth, such as "d." After pronouncing "d," the tongue must move to a slightly higher position to pronounce "t." There are also liquids ("l" sounds), mutes (when "b" sounds "Buh!," it is mute because it is only breath, unlike "bee" which does have voiced sound; same with "c," "k," "d," "g," "p," "t"). Some sounds are nasal, as in "sing." Though not common in English, we may trill a sound or roll an "r." Each of these variations has a potential impact on a poem's sounds. This relatively simple terminology specializing in the physical nature of sound equips us to distinguish sound effectively and know exactly what is happening in a given poem.

Chapter Three

Rhythm

Rhythm is motion. And motion is emotion.

We have spoken of the movement of the voice across and down lines of a poem. We have spoken of the changes of sound through a poem. Rhythm has never been far behind in these topics, since the rhythmic movement of line carries the movement of emotion, just as sound does.

Accompanying rhythm, this chapter includes specific elements of *tempo* (the speed of speaking lines), *pitch* (the relative rise and fall of voice), and *pause*.

Rhythm in poetry is the movement of meaningful sound across the line and from line to line, down through the whole poem. Rhythm is achieved by the *phrasing of our speaking voice*, and by phrasing we mean the movement of the voice through groups of words that cohere because of syntax (e.g., a preposition and its object) or are created by the structure of the line. Rhythmic phrasing encompasses both sound and silence, and as such is carried by a pressure across individual lines and a pressure downward through the entire poem. In short, rhythm expresses meaning.[1]

To begin talking about rhythm, we return to a William Carlos Williams poem to hear how the movement of sound across and down the lines gives meaning and emotion:

> They taste good to her
> They taste good
> to her. They taste
> good to her

If each sentence were spoken alone as a sentence, we would hear only bland repetition, with no rhythm. In chapter one we discussed this poem as an expression of natural speech. To speak the lines is to speak in the rhythms of American speech, for the phrasing of each line gives emphasis and meaning to specific words. The emphasis placed on key words changes with each line; that is, emphasis varies on each "good" in the first four lines.

> They taste good to her
> They taste good
> to her. They taste
> good to her

In the movement across each line we hear both the emphasis that changes in each line and the emotion that is carried in the speaker's voice, chiefly by the repetition and variation of "good" and "her." For what he is stressing is her pleasure. His line breaks create the rhythmic flow, a flow with pauses and varied emphasis.

Rhythm concerns the *manner* of phrasing. That is, we do not give equal emphasis to each accented word or syllable. For example, in a rhythmic presentation of the first two lines of a sonnet by John Milton,

> When I consider how my light is spent,
> E'er half my days, in this dark world and wide,

we would give primary emphasis (all caps) on **LIGHT** and **SPENT**, secondary emphasis (first letter caps) on I and Consider: "when I Consider how my **LIGHT** is **SPENT**." Thus two primary and two secondary emphases, with words of lesser stress, make up the rhythm of the line, that is, how it is being expressed to reveal meaning and emotion, the speaker in the act of considering. In the second line, being somewhat parenthetical, "dark" and "wide," while important, receive less stress than the primary stressed words in line one.

With the variations of emphasis on certain words and therefore variations in the speed by which we speak the lines, when we read these lines of Milton, we are able to hear the rhythmic, emotional content of Milton's speaker as reflective, sober, unresolved.

Implications of Rhythm in Poems

In chapter one, on Line, we called attention to a student's misquotation of Robert Hass's "Heroic Simile" which flattened emphasis. Here is another mistake at least as memorable and valuable. The class was discussing Wilfred Owen's "Dulce et Decorum Est" and one student became convinced the poem was written with a marching rhythm. When asked to demonstrate, he jumped up, walked to the front of the room, and gave a stirring parade-ground exhibition. We were impressed! But after the applause quieted, he confessed his surprise: halfway through his exercise he realized that his steps, as he spoke the words, did not correspond to Owen's rhythms. And I, thinking the point had been made that the poem was not in a marching rhythm, failed to advance the stronger point: "Why does your precision march step *not* correspond to the rhythm of the spoken lines?" A colleague later suggested that Owen's rhythm be called a "defeated heroic," the very human faltering rhythm that contrasts with a mechanical marching posture. Here is the poem:

> Bent double, like old beggars under sacks,
> Knock-kneed, coughing like hags, we cursed through sludge,
> Till on the haunting flares we turned our backs
> And towards our distant rest began to trudge.
> Men marched asleep. Many had lost their boots
> But limped on, blood-shod. All went lame; all blind;
> Drunk with fatigue; deaf even to the hoots
> Of tired, outstripped Five-Nines that dropped behind.
>
> Gas! Gas! Quick, boys! —An ecstasy of fumbling,
> Fitting the clumsy helmets just in time;
> But someone still was yelling out and stumbling,
> And flound'ring like a man in fire or lime . . .
> Dim, through the misty panes and thick green light,
> As under a green sea, I saw him drowning.
>
> In all my dreams, before my helpless sight,
> He plunges at me, guttering, choking, drowning.
>
> If in some smothering dreams you too could pace
> Behind the wagon that we flung him in,

And watch the white eyes writhing in his face,
His hanging face, like a devil's sick of sin;
If you could hear, at every jolt, the blood
Come gargling from the froth-corrupted lungs,
Obscene as cancer, bitter as the cud
Of vile, incurable sores on innocent tongues,—
My friend, you would not tell with such high zest
To children ardent for some desperate glory,
The old Lie: *Dulce et decorum est*
Pro patria mori.

The image of "bent double, like old beggars under sacks" shows us that the soldiers were not spit-and-polish ideals. We *see* that. But as we enter into the rhythm, we go beyond seeing to *experience their experience.* We hear in those first lines a broken, jarring movement. Even the smoother rhythm of "And flound'ring . . . " is part of a dreamed vision before he is suddenly jerked back into the present reality of a staggering rhythm: "He plunges at me, guttering, choking, drowning."

The Nigerian Nobel laureate Wole Soyinka was giving a reading of his poetry (written in English) at our college. The students had been only briefly schooled in the contexts and traditions of his poetry, so one could not be sure how much they would gain from his poems. But after the reading, they were of one mind: even when unable to catch the full intellectual meaning, they *felt* the rhythmic power of his verse.

Practicing Rhythm

How the rhythm of a poem moves may not, of course, be obvious at our first encounter. We may have to practice reading aloud to hear the rhythms, try alternate readings, listen to what seems coherent with line structure, tempo, and the like, until we approximate a normal speech rhythm, even if it may be an unfamiliar one. What complicates rhythmic clarity may be questions like: who is this speaker, what attitude do we hear, what kind of phasing moves through the line structure? To resolve potential difficulties, in, for example, Philip Levine's "What Work Is," we listen first for the way line breaks create voice. Here is the complete poem:

What Work Is

We stand in the rain in a long line
waiting at Ford Highland Park. For work.
You know what work is—if you're
old enough to read this you know what
work is, although you may not do it.
Forget you. This is about waiting,
shifting from one foot to another.
Feeling the light rain falling like mist
into your hair, blurring your vision
until you think you see your own brother
ahead of you, maybe ten places.
You rub your glasses with your fingers,
and of course it's someone else's brother,
narrower across the shoulders than
yours but with the same sad slouch, the grin
that does not hide the stubbornness,
the sad refusal to give in to
rain, to the hours wasted waiting,
to the knowledge that somewhere ahead
a man is waiting who will say, "No,
we're not hiring today," for any
reason he wants. You love your brother,
now suddenly you can hardly stand
the love flooding you for your brother,
who's not beside you or behind or
ahead because he's home trying to
sleep off a miserable night shift
at Cadillac so he can get up
before noon to study his German.
Works eight hours a night so he can sing
Wagner, the opera you hate most,
the worst music ever invented.
How long has it been since you told him
you loved him, held his wide shoulders,
opened your eyes wide and said those words,

and maybe kissed his cheek? You've never
done something so simple, so obvious,
not because you're too young or too dumb,
not because you're jealous or even mean
or incapable of crying in
the presence of another man, no,
just because you don't know what work is.

Already in the slow, steady opening lines, we hear the speaker's tedium of waiting "For work," as if he is speaking to someone unaware of what the wait is for. Whom he addresses then becomes apparent:

You know what work is—if you're
old enough to read this you know what
work is, although you may not do it.

His attitude toward that person is heard in the line break after "you're" that stresses "old enough." So also with the next line: "you know what / work is." The key words might sound like this—but without exaggeration:

You *KNOW* what Work is—if you're
OLD enough to Read this you *KNOW* what
WORK is, although you May not *DO* it.

The annoyance in his speech rhythms intensifies:

Forget you. This is about waiting,
shifting from one foot to another.
Feeling the light rain falling like mist. . . .

The stress on "For-Get You" might sound contemptuous, but perhaps we are not hearing that quite right yet. Then come the stressed participles—waiting, shifting, feeling—that say, this is the experience I am really talking about. Even though the words (line 8) "light rain falling like mist" are gentle, the tone of the speaker remains gruff, with a tension. Were we to accent "**FALL**ing like **MIST** / **INTO** your **HAIR**," the effect would be romantic (too much lilt) and antithetical to the speaker's tone of voice. The speaker's discouragement is more likely carried thus: "**FALL**ing like mist / into your Hair, **BLUR**ring your Vision," the rain making him just plain miserable. Through the poem, we hear the voice of this dispirited

Detroit factory worker who is also a brother, hear his tone that is brusque yet not dismissive (he could have used vulgarity instead of "Forget you"). Such vocal variations prepare for the change to genuine tenderness:

> You love your brother,
>> now suddenly you can hardly stand
>> the love flooding you for your brother,

Levine does not avoid the manifest affection of brothers. We hear his voice rising on the stressed words: "now SUDDENLY you can Hardly STAND / the Love FLOODING you for your BROTHER." To flatten the stress on words and ignore the line structure and rhythm would be to read a mawkish, lifeless poem.

In West Indian poet (born in St. Lucia) Derek Walcott's "The Star-Apple Kingdom" (the final poem of the book *The Star-Apple Kingdom*, 1979), the rhythm speaks of a complex of cultural concerns. The opening lines explore why the landscape of his Caribbean island is invariably deemed inferior to the normative landscape of British painting.

> There were still shards of an ancient pastoral
>> in those shires of the island where the cattle drank
>>> their pools of shadow from an older sky,
>>>> surviving from when the landscape copied such subjects as
> "Herefords at Sunset in the Valley of the Wye."
> The mountain water that fell white from the mill wheel
>> sprinkling like petals from the star-apple trees,
>>> and all of the windmills and sugar mills moved by mules
>>> on the treadmill of Monday to Monday, would repeat
>>> in tongues of water and wind and fire, in tongues
>> of Mission School pickaninnies, like rivers remembering
>> their source, Parish Trelawny, Parish St. David, Parish
> St. Andrew, the names afflicting the pastures,
>> the lime groves and fences of marl stone and the cattle
>> with a docile longing, an epochal content.

The rhythmic pulses (not pauses) are marked out (//) in phrases, "in those shires // of the island // where the cattle drank," so the verse moves ahead, invoking something measured and beautiful—"The mountain water that fell white from the mill wheel / sprinkling like petals from the star-apple trees"—rather than a stolen landscape which no one is taught to respect. The rhythms define a beauty of landscape which has been denied or neglected.

But while "Kingdom" is a long poem, stately in the colors of its imagery, its rhythms also express anguish: we are led to see in an aging photograph "of fine old colonial families . . . "

> [. . .]off at its edges, innocently excluded
> stood the groom, the cattle boy, the housemaid, the gardeners,
> the tenants, the good Negroes down in the village,
> their mouths in the locked jaw of a silent scream.

The words "innocently excluded" hang ominously at line break, and the rhythm changes with the census of the people and their roles, those who made this island, to the irony in "good Negroes"; the ponderous syllables of the last line abruptly halt at "scream."

As he continues, Walcott is constructing beauty as he explores his world's details and celebrates the rhythm of deep seas and stars:

> The mountains rolled like whales through phosphorus stars,
> as he swayed like a stone down fathoms into sleep,
> drawn by that magnet which pulls down half the world
> between a star and a star, by that black power
> that has the assassin dreaming of snow,
> that poleaxes the tyrant to a sleeping child. . . .

Tempo

Since rhythm involves the movement of phrasing across the lines of a poem, the speed with which we speak those lines figures importantly in vocal presentation. Too fast or too slow a tempo can interfere with or negate what a poem says. And there are ways to determine what is too fast or too slow.

Tempo can be defined as *the amount of time it takes to speak* a *word, a line, a stanza, a complete poem.*

The tempo of a *word* is controlled by the number of syllables, the length of the vowels, and the quality of the consonants and vowels. For example, the words "window" and "forests" each require a different duration of time to pronounce because the cluster of consonants in "-ests" slows enunciation. The time it takes to pronounce a vowel or consonant can also change if we elongate it. In the first line of Levine's poem, "We stand in the rain in a long line," "rain" and "long line" elongate to slow the feeling of the line.

In *a line*, tempo is controlled by the number and kind of words, the vocal space or pauses between them, punctuation, and line break. A *stanza's* tempo is controlled by the number of lines with their punctuation, pauses, indentations, and so on. The tempo of a *complete poem* combines the individual parts but also includes a tempo which runs vertically through the whole, the string that binds the entire poem. Tempo, then, offers the beginning of tone, which is the emotion of the poem, the manner and expressive intent by which something is said.

Elements of Tempo

The first two stanzas of William Blake's poem "Tyger" illustrate the spaces we hear between words.

> Tyger, Tyger, burning bright,
> In the Forests of the Night;
> What immortal hand or eye,
> Could frame thy fearful symmetry?
>
> In what distant deeps or skies
> Burnt the fire of thine eyes?
> On what wings dare he aspire?
> What the hand dare seize the fire?

With or without punctuation (an editor's addition), our voice pauses after each "Tyger" and slows as we pronounce "Forests." We articulate the words "hand or eye" to make each distinct. The fourth line moves more steadily with a slight elongation of "frame." The articulate language of the second stanza again controls our deliberate and unhurried tempo so that we hear the import of each word and line.

Greater than usual indentation may change tempo. Here is the opening of Dolores Kendrick's "Leah: in Freedom," one of a series of poems in the voices of slave women:

> I run away
>
>   I keep runnin' away
>
>   they won't let me alone
>
>   they won't let me bear
>
>   my misery to the river
>
>   and out
>
>   over the sky
>
>   or even
>
>   under the trees
>
>   in moles' holes
>
>   and wolves' caves
>
>   and blackberry patches
>
>   with my feet
>
>   skiddin' and bleedin'
>
>   on the thorns
>
>   and then it rains
>
>   on my run
>
>   as quick as my momma's voice
>
>   on the slippery road
>
>   to freedom. . . .

Leah's breathless haste and worry and resentment are heard in her quick, fragmented lines. Her oral repetitions—"I run away / I keep runnin' away"— simulate the tempo, and following "my misery" a series of prepositional phrases speed her on her way until the sudden pause at "on the thorns." While unmarked we hear a break here because a new sentence begins, "and then it rains" that slows the tempo. The line break and space at "to freedom" create a pause in her voice, as if she must not forget the overpowering purpose of her run. In the final lines of the poem, as Leah talks to herself, mimicking her mistress' voice, indentation changes voice and emotion:

> Mistress say 'good mawnin', Leah'
>
>   (won't look at me)
>
>   and tell me about faith
>
>   and Jesus.

The indentation of "(won't look at me)" urges a longer pause and change of voice, as if tossed off under her breath (Kendrick reads "good mawnin', Leah" in a whiny, Mistress voice). The space after "and tell me" is Leah's slight drawing-in of breath before repeating what she was told "about faith." That pause drops heavy stress on "about faith" but more on "and Jesus"—the name is almost blasphemous, for clearly the Mistress has no notion of faith or of Jesus: the complete poem contains the full truth of that.

No single principle confirms how indentation can change tempo. If we return to Charles Olson's "Maximus, to Himself" (chapter one), we hear in this longer selection his complex uses of tempo:

> I have had to learn the simplest things
> last. Which made for difficulties.
> Even at sea I was slow, to get the hand out, or to cross
> a wet deck.
>   The sea was not, finally, my trade.
> But even my trade, at it, I stood estranged
> from that which was most familiar. Was delayed,
> and not content with the man's argument
> that such postponement
> is now the nature of
> obedience,
>   that we are all late
>   in a slow time,
>   that we grow up many
>   And the single
>   is not easily
>   known
>
> It could be, though the sharpness (the *achiote*)
> I note in others,
> makes more sense
> than my own distances. The agilities
>   they show daily
>   who do the world's
>   businesses
>   And who do nature's
>   as I have no sense
>   I have done either . . .

Even in the first long lines tempo creates silences and hesitancies of self-examination. Indentation within stanzas, such as "The sea was not, . . . "

also gestures change. The shortening lines—"is now the nature of / obedi-ence"—prepare for the indented short-lined stanza of greater meditative focus. But tempo in the second indented stanza is different, ironically com-menting on what has been called the prudence of the worldly, which he lacks. For Olson, tempo is obviously central to his poetic.

Here, in the midst of a scene from "Alexander's Feast" (1697), John Dryden varies tempo with great agility:

> Sooth'd with the sound, the King grew vain;
> Fought all his battles o'er again;
> And thrice He routed all his foes, and thrice he slew the slain.
> The Master saw the madness rise;
> His glowing cheeks, his ardent eyes;
> And while He heav'n and earth defy'd,
> Chang'd his hand, and check'd his pride.

The poet Timotheus is playing his lyre and singing for the king, in fact, exploiting his dazzling power over the king's emotions. Even were we not to know the meaning of "Chang'd," the word's sound would slow us. The non-stop tempo of line three parallels the king's excitement with battle, so to rein in these feelings from the madness of war to private sadness, "Chang'd . . . , and check'd" demand careful articulation.

The rhythms of Langston Hughes's "Morning After" have a slangy, per-sonal tone:

> I was so sick last night I
> Didn't hardly know my mind.
> So sick last night I
> Didn't know my mind.
> I drunk some bad licker that
> Almost made me blind.

If we read these lines according to syntax alone, we might be tempted to say something like:

> I was so sick last night // I didn't hardly know my mind.

This may sound fine. But it's not the poem because we have changed the lines and thus tempo, rhythm, meaning. The line reads:

> I was so sick last night I

The voice remains high at line break emphasizing "I / Didn't." The third line is a repeat—well, not exactly. It omits "I was" just as the fourth omits "hardly." The rhythm across the first two lines alerts us to these word-gaps, so our voice must replace the lost syllables by slightly elongating "So sick" and "Didn't know." The pulse of rhythm remains the same even with fewer syllables. The poem goes on like this:

> Had a dream last night I
> Thought I was in hell.
> I drempt last night I
> Thought I was in hell.
> Woke up and looked around me—
> Babe, your mouth was open like a well.
>
> I said, Baby! Baby!
> Please don't snore so loud.
> Baby! Please!
> Please don't snore so loud.
> You jest a little bit o' woman but you
> Sound like a great big crowd.

The rhythm of this poem is based on a musical form, the blues. Blues singers are often less concerned with syllable count than with elongations, pauses, and slurred notes (to fill in a missing word) to suggest meaning. Thus the line break "so sick last night I /" interrupts the syntax for a rhythmic off-beat.

Musical tempo occurs in Gwendolyn Brooks's classic poem:

> *We Real Cool*
>> The Pool Players.
>> Seven at the Golden Shovel.
>
> We real cool. We
> Left school. We
>
> Lurk late. We
> Strike straight. We
>
> Sing sin. We
> Thin gin. We
>
> Jazz June. We
> Die soon.

Again, we may be tempted to read this: "We real Cool / We left school / We lurk late / We . . ." But the lines tell of something different. The period in each line stops the tempo and restarts it emphasizing "We." This off-beat, up-lift stress on "We" at each line-end becomes a finger-snapping jazzy beat which declares the brash attitude of the seven . . . until the last line, when "We" no longer appears, their being dead. And there is more. The tempo moves not only across lines but down the lines. The pause after "We real cool. We" is slighter than the stanza-break after "Left school. We." This stanza pause both interrupts the fluid jazzy beat and partially defeats the players' arrogance, preparing for their (self-acknowledged?) death.

In this next poem, not at all colloquial, Walt Whitman takes us through a wondrous process of confronting death. We hear the rhythmic effects of water and wave and, more specifically, of a rocking cradle. The following passage comes from the conclusion of "Out of the Cradle Endlessly Rocking":

Whereto answering, the sea,
Delaying not, hurrying not,
Whisper'd me through the night, and very plainly before day-break,
Lisp'd to me the low and delicious word death,
And again death, death, death, death,
Hissing melodious, neither like the bird nor like my arous'd child's heart,
But edging near as privately for me rustling at my feet,
Creeping thence steadily up to my ears and laving me softly all over,
Death, death, death, death, death.

The back-and-forth swaying rhythms—"deLAYing not, HURrying not"—achieve a slow tempo that continues to line four with "the low and delicious word death" with a near regularity of unaccent–accent. This accentual sway continues even into the daring repetition of "death," a repetition Whitman risks so that we say each word singly to simulate lisping the "low and delicious word"; the lulling "-th" mutes the hardness of "d," taking the bite out of death. It is this rhythmic flow that we can call incantatory because its chant-like movement becomes mesmerizing. These rhythmic pulses persuade us to accept, even welcome the comforting, unfrightening face of death.

One last example. In "Buffalo Bill's," E. E. Cummings rings amazing variations of tempo on a somber theme, which we present here without commentary:

Buffalo Bill's
defunct
    who used to
        ride a watersmooth-silver
                stallion
and break onetwothreefourfive pigeonsjustlikethat
                            Jesus

he was a handsome man
               and what i want to know is
how do you like your blueeyed boy
Mister Death

Pitch

When vocalizing poems, our voices rise and fall the same way they do in normal speech. This *relative height of voice when we speak* is what we mean by *pitch*. By itself, a word does not have pitch: we do not say "tomato" or "flower" with a distinct pitch. Pitch rises or falls on sounds that differ from surrounding sounds. For instance in the Cummings,

    who used to
        ride a watersmooth-silver
                stallion
and break onetwothreefourfive pigeonsjustlikethat
                            Jesus

he was a handsome man

our voice rises on "stallion," rises more on "pigeons," and more yet on "Jesus." Word placement is key to pitch change here.

    While a flat, unpitched voice may suggest minimal emotion, lines at times may contain only slight pitch variation because the emotion is constrained:

Whose woods these are I think I know,
His house is in the village though;

Pitch lifts on "think" in context of lower vowel sounds, as it does slightly on "village."

In a letter with a number of amusing questions, Robert Frost asked a surprisingly pungent question about the nature of pitch: "Has the word 'Warren' the same vocal value in every one of the four places it occurs in "The Death of the Hired Man?"[2] Vocal value is similar to pitch: the rise or fall of our voice as we say the name.

> Mary sat musing in the lamp-flame at the table
> Waiting for Warren.

> She took the market things from Warren's arms;

> 'Warren,' she said, 'he has come home to die.'

> 'But, Warren, please remember how it is.'

One would scarcely think that a spoken name could change so much. Even in these lines taken out of context, the emphasis and emotional tone are clearly changing. In the third, the pitch rises on "die," and in the last example it rises on **WAR**-ren almost like a warning.

In the first stanzas of Wallace Stevens's "Thirteen Ways of Looking at a Blackbird," pitch may not seem an important factor, but one feels a distinct lift of pitch on the word "blackbird" in the third line of the fourth stanza: "A man and a woman and a blackbird." Like a finger pointing to a central detail, pitch rises on "blackbird" because it is a surprising addition.

Pitch in a Single Poem

For an extended examination of the importance of pitch in a poem, we listen to the opening stanzas of D. H. Lawrence's "Snake":

> A snake came to my water-trough
> On a hot, hot day, and I in pyjamas for the heat,
> To drink there.

> In the deep, strange-scented shade of the great dark carob-tree
> I came down the steps with my pitcher
> And must wait, must stand and wait, for there he was at the trough
>   before me.
> He reached down from a fissure in the earth-wall in the gloom
> And trailed his yellow-brown slackness soft-bellied down, over the edge
>   of the stone trough

And rested his throat upon the stone bottom,
And where the water had dripped from the tap, into a small clearness,
He sipped with his straight mouth,
Softly drank through his straight gums, into his slack long body,
Silently.

In these opening long and short lines (lines six and eight are unbroken) we hear the heavy heat of the day in the aspirated sounds of "hot, hot," and hear the deliberate tempo of the speaker describing his surroundings, his hesitance, the snake's procession, until the stunning one word stop, "Silently." As we begin the third stanza, we start to feel an instinctive snaky motion. Lawrence brings this motion into our bodies through movement of pitch:

　　　　↑　　　↓　　　↑ ↓　　　　↑　　↓ ↑　　　↓
He reached down from a fissure in the earth-wall in the gloom

　　　　　　　　　　　　　　　　　　　　　↓
And trailed his yellow-brown slackness soft-bellied down,

　　　　　　　　　　　　↑　　　↓　　　　　　↓
　　　　　　　　　over the edge of the stone trough

　　　　　　　　　　　　　　↓
And rested his throat upon the stone bottom.

We feel the snake's gradual progress phrase by phrase, for our pitch rises and falls with each phrase: "he **REACHED** down // from a **FIS**-sure // in the **EARTH**-wall // **IN** the gloom." Note, however: pitch need not always lift before dropping; i.e., our marking system may exaggerate the rise. In the next line, pitch does not vary, for the snake is moving forward, but it changes as the snake again descends: "soft-bellied down, / **OVER** the edge // of the stone trough." Pitch and sounds are constant as the snake stops and lies at rest: "rested his throat upon the stone bottom," as again at the end, when he drinks "into his slack long body." The sensations of movement we feel in our voices and bodies come expressly from the phrasing of the lines.

The rest of the poem, a model of line and stanza use, is too beautiful not to quote in full:

Someone was before me at my water-trough,
And I, like a second comer, waiting.

He lifted his head from his drinking, as cattle do,
And looked at me vaguely, as drinking cattle do,

And flickered his two-forked tongue from his lips, and mused a moment,
And stooped and drank a little more,
Being earth-brown, earth-golden from the burning bowels of the earth
On the day of Sicilian July, with Etna smoking.
The voice of my education said to me
He must be killed,
For in Sicily the black, black snakes are innocent, the gold are venomous.

And voices in me said, If you were a man
You would take a stick and break him now, and finish him off.

But must I confess how I liked him,
How glad I was he had come like a guest in quiet, to drink at my
                                                    water-trough
And depart peaceful, pacified, and thankless,
Into the burning bowels of this earth?

Was it cowardice, that I dared not kill him?
Was it perversity, that I longed to talk to him?
Was it humility, to feel so honoured?
I felt so honoured.

And yet those voices:
If you were not afraid, you would kill him!

And truly I was afraid, I was most afraid,
But even so, honoured still more
That he should seek my hospitality
From out the dark door of the secret earth.

He drank enough
And lifted his head, dreamily, as one who has drunken,
And flickered his tongue like a forked night on the air, so black,
Seeming to lick his lips,
And looked around like a god, unseeing, into the air,
And slowly turned his head,
And slowly, very slowly, as if thrice adream,
Proceeded to draw his slow length curving round
And climb again the broken bank of my wall-face.

And as he put his head into that dreadful hole,
And as he slowly drew up, snake-easing his shoulders, and entered farther,
A sort of horror, a sort of protest against his withdrawing into that horrid
                                   black hole,
Deliberately going into the blackness, and slowly drawing himself after,
Overcame me now his back was turned.

I looked round, I put down my pitcher,
I picked up a clumsy log
And threw it at the water-trough with a clatter.

I think it did not hit him,
But suddenly that part of him that was left behind convulsed in
                                 undignified haste,
Writhed like lightning, and was gone
Into the black hole, the earth-lipped fissure in the wall-front,
At which, in the intense still noon, I stared with fascination.

And immediately I regretted it.
I thought how paltry, how vulgar, what a mean act!
I despised myself and the voices of my accursed human education.

And I thought of the albatross,
And I wished he would come back, my snake.

For he seemed to me again like a king,
Like a king in exile, uncrowned in the underworld,
Now due to be crowned again.

And so, I missed my chance with one of the lords
Of life.
And I have something to expiate;
A pettiness.
                                      Taormina, 1923

The narrator admits his fascination with the snake's striking physical-ity: "I liked him," "I felt so honoured." Nevertheless, his intellect rejects the attraction—"I picked up a clumsy log"—because the snake challenges "The voice of my education" which "said to me / He must be killed" as danger-ous (though it is non-poisonous) and darkly sensuous. The movement of pitch reveals the narrator's discovery of animal vitality as his own physical sensations harmonize with the snake's, a response that instigates the conflict with his arid education which denies both body and (ironically) spirit. Realizing how deeply he has internalized the energy of the snake, he cannot but confess finally his "pettiness" and his need "to expiate" his cruel act against the snake.

Pause

We said above that pause was natural to our speech and essential to the speed or tempo of lines, thus to the rhythm of verse. Like line and stanza breaks, pauses can differ both in duration and in quality.

In Thomas Gray's "Elegy Written in a Country Churchyard" none of the first stanza's lines indicate explicit pauses.

> The curfew tolls the knell of parting day,
> The lowing herd wind slowly o'er the lea,
> The ploughman homeward plods his weary way,
> And leaves the world to darkness and to me.

Elongations do slow the first two lines—for example, "knell" and "slowly"—but it is only in the final line where a clear pause occurs: "And leaves the world to darkness and to me," the pause after "darkness" isolating the speaker. Gray runs his lines in nearly uniform tempo so the actual pause gains dramatic meaning.

If pauses are clues to tempo and thus to rhythm, they are instrumental in shaping meaning. We return to a sonnet of John Milton:

> When I consider how my light is spent,
> E'er half my days, in this dark world and wide,
> And that one talent which is death to hide,
> Lodg'd in me useless, though my soul more bent
> To serve therewith my Maker, and present
> My true account, lest he returning chide;
> "Doth God exact day-labor, light denied,"
> I fondly ask; But Patience to prevent
> That murmur, soon replies, "God does not need
> Either man's work or his own gifts; who best
> Bear his mild yoke, they serve him best; his state

> Is Kingly. Thousands at his bidding speed
> And post o'er land and ocean without rest:
> They also serve who only stand and wait."

The first line advances steadily like his mind's search. At the near-parenthetical "in this dark world and wide," pauses enclose the phrase. Each subsequent pause has its own distinct duration and quality as the speaker is increasingly distracted:

> Lodg'd in me useless, though my soul more bent
> To serve therewith my Maker, and present
> My true account, lest he returning chide;
> "Doth God exact day-labor, light denied,"
> I fondly ask. But Patience to prevent . . .

A slight separation even occurs between "Patience" and "to prevent" as she prepares her reply. The concluding two lines of the poem move steadfastly with a beautiful rising of pitch on "stand and wait."

On occasion, the temptation we feel to pause may conflict with the voice's movement through the lines. For instance, we read aloud William Stafford's "Walking the Borders":

> Sometimes in the evening a translator walks out
> and listens by streams that wander back and forth
> across borders. The translator holds a mint
> on the tongue, turns it over to try
> a new side, then tastes a wild new flavor,
> a flavor that enlivens those fading languages
> of cursing and calling each other those names
> that destroyed millions by swinging a cross
> like an ax, or a crescent curved like a knife,
> or a star so red it burned its way over the ground.
>
> The wild new flavor fades away too,
> but lingers awhile along borders for a translator to savor
> secretly, borrowing from both sides, holding
> for a moment the smooth round world
> in that cool instant of evening before the sun goes down.

The thoughtful, languid pace of the opening lines is encouraged by elongating "Sometimes," and "evening," and "by streams." Such elongations do not indicate pauses, only a slowing of the unbroken tempo, with a slight pulse of emphasis on the elongated words. The meditative tone of the line "but lingers awhile . . ." is markedly whole, and the final line again slows meditatively: "evening before the sun goes down."

One final instance of the ways pauses affect a poem's rhythm and meaning. While meaning can be suspended at a pause, sometimes the meaning continues. That is, silence itself can mean.

> I was angry with my friend;
> I told my wrath, my wrath did end.
> I was angry with my foe:
> I told it not, my wrath did grow.

In this first stanza of William Blake's "The Poison Tree," we hear five pauses, each with a different and distinct expectation. "I was angry with my friend"—a silence awaits disclosure. At "I was angry with my foe," the silence is weightier because the consequence begins to be dangerous. The hesitance after "I told it not" is very ominous, and then "my wrath did grow" promises something alarming. Stanza two takes on the quick urgency of glee, accentuated by the repetitions of "And":

> And I watered it in fears,
> Night and morning with my tears:
> And I sunned it with smiles,
> And with soft deceitful wiles.
>
> And it grew both day and night,
> Till it bore an apple bright.
> And my foe beheld it shine,
> And he knew that it was mine.
>
> And into my garden stole,
> When the night had veiled the pole;
> In the morning glad I see
> My foe outstretched beneath the tree.

The silence after "it was mine" is deeply disturbing for the foe's motivation is not disclosed, nor is his action, though we imagine that like Adam in the

Garden, he eats. The pauses are stunningly cruel in the culminating lines: "In the morning glad I see / . . ."

Notes

1 Being fundamental to human cycles and relationships, rhythm can be considered, as poet Czeslaw Milosz says, "the highest earthly expression of what is called thought." This is not just a Western concept. Senegalese poet and statesman Léopold Senghor defined rhythm in "Ce que l'homme noir apporte" (1939):

> It is the thing that is most perceptible and least material. . . . It is the first condition and the hallmark of Art, as breath is of life: breath, which accelerates or slows, which becomes even or agitated according to the tension in the individual, the degree and the nature of his emotion. . . . It is not the kind of symmetry that gives rise to monotony; rhythm is alive, it is free. . . . This is how rhythm affects what is least intellectual in us, tyrannically, to make us penetrate to the spirituality of the object, and that character of abandon which is ours is itself rhythmic.

2 *Robert Frost on Writing,* ed. Elaine Barry. (New Brunswick, NJ: Rutgers University Press, 1973), 75.

Chapter Four

Meter

M eter is *the measure of a repeated pattern of word accents. Repeated* and *pattern* are the important terms. The difference between *meter* and *rhythm* (in the previous chapter) is evident in the words' origins: *rhythm* comes from the Greek for "motion or movement," and *meter* derives from the Greek word for "measure." While both terms indicate an abstract concept, both also imply a physicality, a bodily quality important in speaking and hearing poetry.

To observe meter, we listen for the natural fall of word accents to find what patterns appear, such as accent–unaccent, unaccent–accent, two accents–unaccent, or the opposite. For example, to return to the opening lines of Stanley Kunitz's "End of Summer," the accent pattern might look like this:

> an **AG**-i-**TA**-tion **OF** the **AIR**,
> a **PER**-tur-**BA**-tion **OF** the **LIGHT**
> ad-**MON**-ished **ME** the **UN**-loved **YEAR**
> would **TURN** on its **HINGE** that **NIGHT**.

Except for the slight variant "on its **HINGE**" in the last line (one less syllable), the lines hold a regular pattern of unaccent–accent syllables. That means that in each line there is a regularly repeating pattern of accents. The lines therefore are metrical. Meter signifies a regularity of beat, like a heartbeat, like a drum or bass beat in music. All multisyllable words have accents, and one-syllable words are accented depending on their use in a sentence, such as "on its **HINGE**" but also "**OF the AIR**."

Metrical regularity in verse settles the lines in a kind of order, poetry's own order that we can hear even if the regular beat is not obvious. Metrical orderliness does not mean, of course, that the poem cannot be about something chaotic. For instance, William Butler Yeats's "The Second Coming" describes the impending collapse of civilization (from the first stanza):

> The blood-dimmed tide is loosed, and everywhere
> The ceremony of innocence is drowned;
> The best lack all conviction, while the worst
> Are full of passionate intensity.

Apart from slight variation in line two, the metrical quality of the lines (ten syllables) do nothing to mitigate the horror of disaster. Such orderliness is that of the poet's art, not of the subject.

Taking account of the pattern of word accents in "End of Summer" or "The Second Coming" or any poem is a practice called *scansion*. Scansion, or scanning, is a method to place accentual patterns into distinct kinds of meter—the predominant meter in "End of Summer" and "The Second Coming" is iambic. (See note for the terminology of the kinds of meter: iamb, trochee, dactyl, anapest.[1])

In a selection of lines from quite different poets, we find the same iambic pattern of unaccented and accented syllables:

> when I con-**SID**-er **HOW** my **LIGHT** is **SPENT**
> (John Milton)

> by **THIS** he **KNEW** she **WEPT** with **WAK**-ing **EYES**
> (George Meredith)

> it **SEEMED** that **OUT** of **BAT**-tle I e-**SCAPED**
> (Wilfred Owen)

> whose **WOOD**s these **ARE** i **THINK** i **KNOW**
> (Robert Frost)

> now **WIN**-ter **DOWNS** the **DY**-ing **OF** the **YEAR**
> (Richard Wilbur)

> be-**TWEEN** my **FIN**-ger **AND** my **THUMB**
> (Seamus Heaney)

Similarity of meter in these lines does not mean similarity of tempo moving across the line or similarity of emphasis on accents. For instance, we read Milton's line with a quite steady movement—"when I con-SID-er HOW my LIGHT is SPENT." In Meredith's line, however—"by THIS he KNEW she WEPT with WAK-ing EYES"—a slight slowing occurs at the elongated "knew" and stress increases on "waking." Same iambic meter, different tempo. In Owen's line—"it SEEMED that OUT of BAT-tle I e-SCAPED"—"seemed" is slightly elongated. Wilbur's "now WIN-ter DOWNS the DY-ing OF the YEAR" has yet its own pattern of expression: stress falls on "DY-ing OF the YEAR." In Heaney's line "be-TWEEN my FIN-ger AND my THUMB," the two nouns receive greater accent. Within the same iambic meter each line is distinct in tempo and in numbers of stressed syllables.

While meter provides patterning and thus a certain orderliness in verse, it allows full variety of expression which we hear when we speak the lines aloud. That is, in speaking poems, we do not ordinarily stress every accented syllable. Such a conspicuous bounce would sound alien to normal speech and introduce a possibly false sing-songiness. That is, we do not give equal stress to the accented words "be-TWEEN my FIN-ger AND my THUMB" but rather let emphasis fall on key words "finger" and "thumb." The meter resides beneath the rhythmic phrasing, present but not forced.

Meter involves both a basic *repeating* pattern, such as iambic, and a *variation* on that pattern. The repeating pattern provides the metrical sameness, but difference is created by changes of stress and by elongation. Without such variation, the movement of our voice across these six lines would sound very similar, as if with a distinct emotion and meaning. While a poem may be written in iambic meter, variation and flexibility of emotion and meaning are entirely consistent with a set metrical pattern. If what we are saying here about variation of accent and elongation appears to be similar to what was said about rhythm, yes, there are similarities: while regularity of accent pattern applies to the nature of meter, variations by stress and elongation constitute an aspect of rhythm.

Changes of Meter

While attention to meter assures us that we hear a patterning of accent in the lines, such attention also alerts us to *variations or changes in metrical regularity* that may signify a change of meaning and emotion. That is, what appears to be an iambic pattern can change.

In William Shakespeare's Sonnet 65, not only does meter vary but the variation is central to the poem's emotional meaning.

> Since brass, nor stone, nor earth, nor boundless sea,
> But sad mortality o'er-sways their power,
> How with this rage shall beauty hold a plea,
> Whose action is no stronger than a flower?
> O how shall summer's honey breath hold out
> Against the wrackful siege of batt'ring days,
> When rocks impregnable are not so stout,
> Nor gates of steel so strong, but Time decays?
> O fearful meditation: Where, alack,
> Shall Time's best jewel from Time's chest lie hid?
> Or what strong hand can hold his swift foot back,
> Or who his spoil of beauty can forbid?
>> O none, unless this miracle have might,
>> That in black ink my love may still shine bright.

Because the opening line seems to begin "Since **BRASS** . . . ," we might assume (a natural enough tendency) that the line remains iambic: "nor **STONE**, nor **EARTH**, nor **BOUND**-less **SEA**." But in order to introduce the negative that is not present in "Since" (possibly stress on both first words), we emphasize "nor" and thus change the meter from iambic.

> Since **BRASS**, **NOR** stone, **NOR** earth, **NOR** bound-less **SEA**

Each "nor" strengthens the emphasis, as the range of barriers grows from a simple piece of brass to the entire sea. The changes of meter as well as changes in strength of accent across the line lift a flat-sounding line (as if it were straight iambic) to one of strong conviction. And this stress on the negatives is part of the meaning of the poem: that is, emphasis falls not so much on the objects as on the negation of them. We hear negatives throughout the poem:

> Whose action is *no* stronger than a flower? . . .
> When rocks impregnable are *not* so stout,
> *Nor* gates of steel so strong, but Time decays? . . .
>
> O *none,* unless this miracle have might, . . .

Along with plays on strength or "might" against the apparent weakness of beauty, flower, love, stress on the negative terms (accent on "not," "Nor" and "none") supports the paradox (reversing the usual) of my love shining bright in "black ink"—a miracle indeed! Even the added syllable in "pow-er" and "flow-er," a weaker, falling-off sound, identify the words that seem opposed but that are finally allied.

A fine example of regularity and variation, Sonnet 65 is, as a consequence, a wonderfully rich and revealing poem to speak aloud. While the opening iamb changes to trochees to accentuate "nor," the nouns are, as we have said, obviously important. The weight placed upon each word in this line is continued through the poem so that there are remarkably few words that are not distinctly pronounced. Perhaps, especially, each word of the final five lines must be read with slow deliberation, with, one might say, nearly equal stress on each word: "Shall Time's best jewel from Time's chest lie hid?" [2]

John Keats's "La Belle Dame sans Merci" is written in ballad stanza with a rhyme scheme ABCB; the lines run 8, 8, 8, 4 syllables:

> O what can ail thee, knight-at-arms,
>   Alone and palely loitering?
> The sedge has withered from the lake
>   And no birds sing.

As we listen to the regular and soulful iambic meter, each word in the truncated last line resists an iambic lilt and frustrates our metrical expectation. The prior line's regular pattern of accent is cut off by the four lurching monosyllables, so what may seem to be flattened expression actually intensifies the desolation of the scene. As we continue "La Belle," we hear Keats create variety in the iambic meter by multiple changes: the second stanza seems repetitive until the positive assertions of lines 3 and 4 challenge the knight's woebegone posture:

> O what can ail thee, knight at arms,
>   So haggard and so woebegone?
> The squirrel's granary is full,
>   And the harvest's done.

Unlike "woebegone," "full" is firmly accented, and line 4 has an extra syllable which accents "done" without the despairing fall. We continue the poem:

I see a lily on thy brow,
　　With anguish moist and fever dew,
And on thy cheek a fading rose
　　Fast withereth too.

Tempo slows with elongated words like "anguish moist," "cheeks," "rose," as also on "withereth." When the knight replies to the narrator, his speech is breathless with mid-line pauses:

I met a lady in the meads
　　Full beautiful—a fairy's child,
Her hair was long, her foot was light,
　　And her eyes were wild.

He luxuriates then with more assured lines in his fancied encounter with the fairy (the rest of poem continues):

I set her on my pacing steed,
　　And nothing else saw all day long,
For sidelong would she bend and sing
　　A fairy's song.

I made a garland for her head,
　　And bracelets too, and fragrant zone;
She looked at me as she did love,
　　And made sweet moan.

She found me roots of relish sweet,
　　And honey wild, and manna-dew,
And sure in language strange she said—
　　"I love thee true."

She took me to her elfin grot,
　　And there she wept and sighed full sore,
And there I shut her wild, wild eyes
　　With kisses four.

And there she lullèd me asleep,
　　And there I dreamed—Ah! woe betide!—
The latest dream I ever dreamt
　　On the cold hill side.

> I saw pale kings and princes too,
>> Pale warriors, death-pale were they all;
> Who cried—"La Belle Dame sans Merci,
>> Thee hath in thrall!"
>
> I saw their starved lips in the gloam,
>> With horrid warning gapèd wide,
> And I awoke and found me here,
>> On the cold hill's side.
>
> And this is why I sojourn here,
>> Alone and palely loitering,
> Though the sedge is withered from the lake,
>> And no birds sing.

At stanza nine his imagined affair has dried up and his lines break down—"Ah, woe betide!" The remarkable variation of the basic iambic that Keats achieves in this poem dramatizes the knight's pathetic condition in his own words, even reiterating the narrator's words at the end to affirm his despair. Metrical regularity may dominate, but variations of meter by altered stress and elongation reveal a full emotional range.

It is hard to resist adding that in this rich and fascinating poem meaning and sound and tempo harmonize with meter to explore emotional complexity, much involved as the ballad is with the role and mental condition of the knight. The metrical tension—like the story itself—leads us to wonder: Is this knight acting a complete fool in denying his knightly vocation? What kind of being is this fairy? What is the meaning of her "sweet moan," of his "kisses four," of her three gifts of roots, honey, and manna? Is nature dead or only in its seasonal cycle?

It is also hard to resist talking about metrical effects in another poem that also happens to be about dwelling with fairies. William Butler Yeats's "The Stolen Child" is a marvelously seductive poem about dreams of an alternate world that is free of this world's pains. Here, too, we find variations of meter and of line length for effect.

> Where dips the rocky highland
> Of Sleuth Wood in the lake,
> There lies a leafy island
> Where flapping herons wake

The drowsy water-rats;
There we've hid our faery vats,
Full of berries
And of reddest stolen cherries.
Come away, O human child!
To the waters and the wild
With a faery, hand in hand,
For the world's more full of weeping than you can understand.

Where the wave of moonlight glosses
The dim grey sands with light,
Far off by furthest Rosses
We foot it all the night,
Weaving olden dances,
Mingling hands and mingling glances
Till the moon has taken flight;
To and fro we leap
And chase the frothy bubbles,
While the world is full of troubles
And is anxious in its sleep.
Come away, O human child!
To the waters and the wild
With a faery, hand in hand,
For the world's more full of weeping than you can understand.

Where the wandering water gushes
From the hills above Glen-Car,
In pools among the rushes
That scarce could bathe a star,
We seek for slumbering trout
And whispering in their ears
Give them unquiet dreams;
Leaning softly out
From ferns that drop their tears
Over the young streams.
Come away, O human child!

To the waters and the wild
With a faery, hand in hand,
For the world's more full of weeping than you can understand.

Away with us he's going,
The solemn-eyed:
He'll hear no more the lowing
Of the calves on the warm hillside
Or the kettle on the hob
Sing peace into his breast,
Or see the brown mice bob
Round and round the oatmeal-chest.
For he comes, the human child,
To the waters and the wild
With a faery, hand in hand,
From a world more full of weeping than he can understand.

It takes but a few lines to hear that these are not regulation iambics—seven-syllable lines make iambs impossible anyway. The first line's steady fall of accent is quickly troubled by line two. It would be awkward to say "of **SLEUTH** wood **IN** the **LAKE**" since we elongate both "Sleuth" and "Wood," and "in" is scarcely stressed before "lake." We trot along quite merrily (metrically) through "Where flapping herons wake" no doubt expecting "wake" to modify herons—but at the line-break the sentence continues. They in fact wake the "drowsy water rats." Not so pleasant an image, these rats!

Where dips the rocky highland
Of Sleuth Wood in the lake,
There lies a leafy island
Where flapping herons wake
The drowsy water-rats;

If seduction is the intent of these fairies, we have been warned by metrical disorder, by "Sleuth Wood," by "water-rats." Of course the clever fairies quickly distract us with delicious pictures "Full of berries" (a curiously shortened line) and "reddest stolen cherries."

The fairies' chant is seductive because the world is indeed *"more full of weeping than you can understand."* If we are tempted, then, to escape this world and leap into the fairy's world of ideal bliss, both their metrical slight-of-hand and their fanciful images ought to give us reason to rethink their offer, to realize their fraudulence.

> He'll hear no more the lowing
> Of the calves on the warm hillside
> Or the kettle on the hob
> Sing peace into his breast,
> Or see the brown mice bob
> Round and round the oatmeal-chest.

The duplicitous world of fairy dreams is no match for Yeats's metrical magic. He outwits them by undermining their chant—even their vision of the cozy world the child abandons is metrically disturbed.

We have made the point that we do not stress each metrical accent because doing so would sound unnatural or affected. And that remains essentially true. Nevertheless, poets like to confuse our neat pronouncements, so some will encourage accenting the full metric beat as an essential part of the verse effect. For example, here is the beginning of Henry Wadsworth Longfellow's "The Song of Hiawatha":

> Should you ask me, whence these stories?
> Whence these legends and traditions,
> With the odors of the forest,
> With the dew and damp of meadows,
> With the curling smoke of wigwams,
> With the rushing of great rivers,
> With their frequent repetitions,
> And their wild reverberations
> As of thunder in the mountains?

While we often *hear* a poem's metrical pattern without consciously noticing it, in this poem we do attend to the metrical pattern as the primary pattern of stress. Repeating "With" to emphasize nouns is certainly part of Longfellow's intended repetitive structure, like an incantation that stacks detail upon detail in the manner of ancient oral chants. The meter accords with the poem's rhythm. In another of Longfellow's poems, a different meter sounds just as consciously regular:

> Often I think of the beautiful town
>> That is seated by the sea;
> Often in thought go up and down
>> The pleasant streets of that dear old town.
>>>> ("My Lost Youth")

What begins with a sedately slow, reflective meter (three syllables: "**OF**-ten i **THINK** of the **BEAU**-ti-ful **TOWN**"), these dactyls set a pace and tone which then becomes mixed with various two-syllable feet and extra syllables. In both of these poems by Longfellow, meter is a strong presence that creates his (possibly sentimental) scene.

Speaking Metrical Verse

At times a poet may challenge our confidence in hearing meter and in speaking verses well. As we read aloud William Blake's "The Chimney Sweeper" (from *Songs of Innocence*), we listen for changes of accent pattern:

> A little black thing among the snow,
> Crying "weep," "weep" in notes of woe!
> "Where are thy father and mother, say?"
> "They are both gone up to the church to pray."

The opening line may sound close to regular iambic: a **LIT**-tle **BLACK** thing a-**MONG** the **SNOW**. But as we speak the words, do we say "**BLACK** thing" or "black **THING**," or "**BLACK THING**"? The regular-seeming meter appears to break down. After "**CRY**-ing," do we read "weep, **WEEP**," or "weep, weep," or "**WEEP, WEEP**"? If we insist on forcing regular patterns of accent onto the lines, our voices may become contorted and lose all sense of meaningful speech. What finally matters is that we speak the lines to recreate and reveal their meaning in the rhythms of speech. Irregularity of accent is part of the impact of the poem: Blake leads us into a difficult, frightening world that challenges an easy read.

Continuing with Blake a moment longer, the regular meter in some of his songs like "London" (iambic),

> I wander thro' each charter'd street
> Near where the chartered Thames does flow;

is unlike that in others (trochaic):

> Tyger, Tyger burning bright
> In the forests of the night;
> > "The Tyger"

or in,

> Little Lamb who made thee?
> Dost thou know who made thee?
> > "The Lamb"

The iamb being practically the standard of English usage, we might suppose that it would be appropriate for a nice, normal Song-of-Innocence lamb. But no. Here are trochees. And if the same trochees express the "Tyger" (albeit the tiger gets one more syllable per line), does that suggest a similarity between lambs and tigers? Should not a frightening poem like "London" be cast in some strange, disjointed meter? Blake used iambics for some lyrics, trochees for others, and varied meter in yet others. The differences are significant, part of the overall design for his *Songs*.

Earlier (in chapter two), we spoke of Wallace Stevens's exploration of consonants in "A High-Toned Old Christian Woman." But here, his metrical fancywork is at least as much fun to listen to.

> Poetry is the supreme fiction, madame.
> Take the moral law and make a nave of it
> And from the nave build haunted heaven. Thus,
> The conscience is converted into palms,
> Like windy citherns hankering for hymns.
> We agree in principle. That's clear. But take
> The opposing law and make a peristyle,
> And from the peristyle project a masque
> Beyond the planets. Thus, our bawdiness,
> Unpurged by epitaph, indulged at last,
> Is equally converted into palms,
> Squiggling like saxophones. And palm for palm,
> Madame, we are where we began. Allow,
> Therefore, that in the planetary scene
> Your disaffected flagellants, well-stuffed,

Smacking their muzzy bellies in parade,
Proud of such novelties of the sublime,
Such tink and tank and tunk-a-tunk-tunk,
May, merely may, madame, whip from themselves
A jovial hullabaloo among the spheres.
This will make widows wince. But fictive things
Wink as they will. Wink most when widows wince.

The first line moves toward metrical regularity so that we feel comfortable pronouncing the words "**FIC**-tion, **MA**-dame." But later in the poem, our tendency to follow a predominant metrical pattern leads us to a surprising change:

like **SAX**-o-**PHONES**. and **PALM** for **PALM**
ma-**DAME**, we **ARE** where **WE** be-**GAN**.

What started as "**MA**-dame" becomes by metrical alteration "ma-**DAME**," Stevens's nice teasing twist!

Notes

1. Here in summary are details about meter. The physicality of poetry, evident in word origins of rhythm and meter, remains constant. There is physicality in "flow or movement" and "measure." The word "foot" likewise once meant the movement of the foot as it beat time for the dance.

    The term *foot* means a set of syllables of one or more words which make up one segment of a metrically accented pattern. Thus, meter is the pattern of repeating *feet*. That is, a group of unaccent/accent syllables constitutes a foot: the two syllables are part of a distinct pattern. In English speech, unaccented and accented syllables will regularly appear next to each other, but to create a foot, there has to be a repeated pattern, a base upon which there may be variants. For example, after three unaccent–accent feet there may be a change to accent–unaccent, but usually the base pattern returns as the dominant. To say that a pentameter line is made up of five feet means the line has five sets of two syllables, or ten syllables ("pentameter" usually implies iambic/trochaic lines). If the two syllables have a pattern of unaccent–accent, we call that foot *iambic* or an *iamb*. The accent is either the natural accent on a syllable, such as "obSERVE," or drawn from context, such as "to SERVE," the verb receiving accent. Since single-syllable words have no natural accent, in a series of one-syllable words, the word group into which they fall usually determines accent: e.g., prepositional phrases or infinitives in which the noun or verb is accented—"to the HOUSE," "on the HILL," "to CATCH." Of course, there are regional variants in pronunciation and accent: De-TROIT is an iamb, but some pronounce it DE-troit. British pronunciation, as in "la-BOR-a-try," "al-u-MIN-i-um, may also be unfamiliar in the United States.

Two-syllable feet are *iamb* (unaccent–accent), *trochee* (accent–unaccent), or *spondee* (accent–accent). Three-syllable feet are *anapest* (two unaccent–accent) or *dactyl* (accent–two unaccent). Lines are named by numbers of feet per line: pentameter has five feet; tetrameter has four feet, trimeter three, and so on. There can be two- or three-syllable feet for each of these line types, though obviously a line of five dactyls would run to fifteen syllables, quite a mouthful (Kinnell gave us a thirteen-syllable line; William Blake used a fourteen-syllable line in his prophetic poems like *Milton*). The iamb is the most common foot in English, practically the normative foot of the language.

Here are examples of each foot:

> Iambic: Whose WOODS these ARE i THINK i KNOW
> Trochee: DOUB-le, DOUB-le, TOIL and TROUB-le
> Anapest: The asSYR-ian came DOWN like a WOLF on the FOLD
> Dactyl: THIS is the FOR-est pri-ME-val
> Spondee: Oh dark, DARK, DARK, amid the blaze of noon

2. Were each word equally accented, the foot could not be called iamb or trochee. It would be a *spondee*: accent–accent. Determining such a difference is not an absolute science but a reader's judgment on how, according to the context, accents should fall.

Chapter Five

Imagery

*A*n image is a depiction in words of a sensory experience. An image appeals to our senses—hearing, sight, taste, touch, smell—and to the intellect as well. We do not of course physically see or feel as a result of an image: it evokes a sensory memory or response and we imagine that we in fact touch or taste or smell. When we read or hear certain words, a picture or image appears in our minds and a sense responds, identifying the object(s). An image can be a reference to a single object or sensation; it can evoke multiple sensory appeals; if repeated, it can develop a *pattern* of imagery through a work.

An image often functions in two stages. We perceive the object exactly, and we apply what is precise in it to something abstract; the actual object leads us to grasp a facet of the non-concrete thing.

Poet Ted Kooser said recently, relative to ineffective teaching of poetry, that he had been taught to fall "upon poems as if they were walnuts we had to crack—rather than seeing poems as pleasurable experiences that we can take into our lives." [1] Because he wanted to examine the abstract thing, "teaching," in practical terms, Kooser placed the abstraction in the context of a concrete object. The walnut gives us an object to see, feel, perhaps hear. It is assumed we know what a walnut is and how to crack it. Kooser's image sets a known action (cracking nuts) against an abstraction (teaching poems) in order to underline the differences between poems and nuts, teaching and cracking.

Words have a literal *denotation*, what they actually mean (a walnut), and words have *connotations*, associated meanings, such as *home* denoting *a structure* and connoting *comfort*. Since words mean in several ways, in reading poetry (or any literature) we must be tuned to such layering of meanings. Many words have multiple denotations. Take, for example, rock: a hard mineral substance; a form of popular music; to create motion, as in a chair, or a boat. But what does rock *connote*? As a hard substance it could suggest a person of solid character. Or one who is block-headed. As action, rocking is moving fast and hard to music (current slang may add more). Because "tide" denotes rising and receding ocean water, it readily connotes a similar reciprocal process in people, events, things: the tides of battle.

Words, objects, emotions, and experiences have meanings beyond the literal. When we hear "My love is like a red red rose," we are quite sure this is not the effusion of a wildly confused gardener. A real linkage exists between red rose and lover that develops multiple associations of the flower and one's love: its passionate redness, its sweet fragrance, its delicacy and perhaps impermanence, its texture of layered petals suggestive of female genitals. If one has no red rose at hand, a yellow or white one will not be the same, for each color has its own signification. Yellow can mean "let's make up again" or it can mean infidelity. A rose can also stand for, be an emblem of warring English families: the red rose of Lancaster, the white of York.

Image and Sensory Appeal

In reading an image we first understand what object(s) it refers to (walnut?). Then, we find the relationship being made between object and referent. If we do not know what the object is or what connection is being formed, the image will have no effect. Finally, we observe how the image moves and develops through the poem.

We will begin with the imagery in Robert Frost's sonnet "Design":

> I found a dimpled spider, fat and white,
> On a white heal-all, holding up a moth
> Like a white piece of rigid satin cloth—
> Assorted characters of death and blight
> Mixed ready to begin the morning right,
> Like the ingredients of a witches' broth—
> A snow-drop spider, a flower like a froth,
> And dead wings carried like a paper kite.

What had that flower to do with being white,
The wayside blue and innocent heal-all?
What brought the kindred spider to that height,
Then steered the white moth thither in the night?
What but design of darkness to appall?—
If design govern a thing so small.

We can visualize the "fat spider"—its being "dimpled" may suggest it is in some way baby-cute. The "heal-all" being normally a blue flower, its dead whiteness is a telling alteration. Frost's images expand: a moth (usually white) is like white (but rigid) satin, so it and the flower and the spider begin to mean or say something; they are "characters," signs that signify or connote something. The collection of objects changes then into witches' brew: "snow-drop spider," "flower like a froth," "wings . . . paper kite," emblems of "death and blight."

Once we see how each is placed together in seemingly unnatural conjunction, the second stanza draws the consequences of the images. Was this assortment of "white" only random or could it have been "brought" together as a deliberate construct by a sinister agent of "darkness"?

In his Sonnet 73, Shakespeare intends his readers to understand that visible signs of nature's change are like stages of aging.

That time of year thou mayst in me behold
When yellow leaves, or none, or few, do hang
Upon those boughs which shake against the cold,
Bare ruined choirs, where late the sweet birds sang.
In me thou see'st the twilight of such day
As after sunset fadeth in the west,
Which by and by black night doth take away,
Death's second self that seals up all in rest.
In me thou seest the glowing of such fire
That on the ashes of his youth doth lie,
As the death-bed whereon it must expire,
Consumed with that which it was nourished by.
   This thou perceiv'st, which makes thy love more strong,
   To love that well which thou must leave ere long.

An English reader would be familiar with yellow leaves and bare branches, would recall the birds that sang last summer, and know from attending Anglican services how choir stalls are arranged. People of non-northern climates might not instantly picture the autumnal loss of leaves, and those with no experience of large European churches might not know what kind of choir is meant (not a chorus).

In this quiet poem—the birds, the fading light, the last ashes are all silent—Shakespeare instructs us carefully: in the image of twilight we are asked to see light of a precise time, color, tone: "of such day / As after sunset fadeth in the west." As the sun departs and the grand blaze is gone, colors mute and blend. This delicate visual tonality is as exact as the other images, the remembrance of "sweet" birds, the "glowing of such fire." As the speaker says, "This thou perceiv'st": we read the images by perceiving specifics of the objects in order to identify something fresh and distinct about the stages of living and loving.

If we are acquainted with an object, a poet may ask us not to rest with that knowledge but to imagine the thing afresh, as if for the first time, to gain new insight. We know, for example, what a home radiator is. When Martin Espada pictures it, he wants us to grasp something beyond what it looks like:

> I cannot evict them
> from my insomniac nights,
> tenants in the city of coughing
> and dead radiators.
> They bang the radiators
> like cold hollow marimbas; . . .

Espada localizes the radiators in the city where tenant evictions and insomnia are common, and warmth is rare. The radiator image takes a turn with "marimba," with its cultural associations (it is not a Glockenspiel). A radiator may look metal and we know it is hollow, but the image expands to the auditory. By placing "cold hollow" next to "radiators" we hear the irony of their sounding like marimbas, just as disparate things like "coughing" and "dead" are associated with a metal object. Espada's images are distinctly audial.

Wallace Stevens's "A High-Toned Old Christian Woman" asks us to follow the images but also to listen for something more in them. His title provides context for the accumulated images, and religious associations are combined with certain sounds of that culture:

A High-Toned Old Christian Woman

Poetry is the supreme fiction, madame.
Take the moral law and make a nave of it
And from the nave build haunted heaven. Thus,
The conscience is converted into palms,
Like windy citherns hankering for hymns.
We agree in principle. That's clear. But take
The opposing law and make a peristyle,
And from the peristyle project a masque
Beyond the planets. Thus, our bawdiness,
Unpurged by epitaph, indulged at last,
Is equally converted into palms,
Squiggling like saxophones. And palm for palm,
Madame, we are where we began. Allow,
Therefore, that in the planetary scene
Your disaffected flagellants, well-stuffed,
Smacking their muzzy bellies in parade,
Proud of such novelties of the sublime,
Such tink and tank and tunk-a-tunk-tunk,
May, merely may, madame, whip from themselves
A jovial hullabaloo among the spheres.
This will make widows wince. But fictive things
Wink as they will. Wink most when widows wince.

In addition to the poem's sound effects, in the opening lines we hear the bold (almost condescending) tone of voice addressing her as "madame," as well as in the assertive lecturing: "Take" and "Thus, . . ."

Poetry is the supreme fiction, madame.
Take the moral law and make a nave of it
And from the nave build haunted heaven. Thus, . . .

We both *hear* the superior tone and *see* the images. The church imagery —nave, heaven, palms, hymns—leads to religious considerations of "moral law," "conscience converted," "citherns." Then the church turns into a temple with a peristyle. The title too helps us draw the stacked images into an assemblage of satiric meaning: this "high-toned old Christian woman" would doubtless view a (pagan!) temple with horror, and even more so the carnality of "hankering" or "bawdiness."

We hear aspirate heavy-breathing in "hankering for hymns" (or "him"). Worse yet in her mind are the anti-liturgical saxophones, and the dangerous physical contact of palm to palm (a multiple pun: hands, trees, Palm Sunday, Romeo and Juliet's courtship dance). The sublime, which is often connected with the spiritual, is now nonsense noise: "Such tink and tank and tunk-a-tunk-tunk." Stevens so deftly expands the visual and audial imagery through his poem that we hear the exact movement of imagery and its mocking tone.

Following the Image: An Analysis

It can happen, of course, that we miss an image, or one image seems unrelated to the next one. Such problems do not necessarily signify a poet's or a reader's failure. In such a case we may have to follow the imagery and trust it will come to meaning. Initially that involves observing the denotations and connotations of each image. Here, for instance, is the opening stanza of Robert Bly's "My Father's Wedding, 1924":

> Today, lonely for my father, I saw
> a log, or branch,
> long, bent, ragged, bark gone.
> I felt lonely for my father when I saw it.
> It was the log
> that lay near my uncle's old milk wagon.

If we say that an image connects a sensible object to something abstract, "log" does not seem to relate to loneliness. Then there is the uncle, and his milk wagon, which also seem to be unconnected to anything so far. (Not to mention that Bly was born in 1926, which means he did not actually attend the wedding.) Unlike Shakespeare's movement of image to image, Bly's images seem to leap about unaccountably.

Bly's speaker feels a question rise up in him: Seeing this log, why do I feel lonely for my father? The answer lies in his (and our) following the image as it gathers associations with other images. The next stanza jumps further ahead and the log becomes a leg (which may suggest a wooden leg):

> Some men live with an invisible limp,
> stagger, or drag
> a leg. Their sons are often angry.

> Only recently I thought:
> Doing what you want . . .
> Is that like limping? Tracks of it show in sand.

But something else is happening: we *hear* this imagery. As we speak or listen to these lines, the pauses and line breaks sound dislocated and un-rhythmical. They stagger:

> Today, lonely for my father, I saw
> a log, or branch,
> long, bent, ragged, bark gone.

The visual becomes distinctly audial, both creating meaning.

At first, the image of limping is bodily, but with the adjective "invisible," it becomes non-physical, an internal defect. The speaker's tangle of associa-tion asks if his own "limp" (admitting that he shares one with his father) is in his anger or in "doing what you want."

There seems no logical reason why stanza three should begin:

> Have you seen those giant bird-
> men of Bhutan?
> Men in bird masks, with pig noses, dancing,

These images appear out of the blue, another leap of time and place which, again, we hear in the line breaks that disconcert our ears. We hear, better than see, those leaps which suggest that random links of images will even-tually coalesce.

> . . . with pig noses, dancing,
> teeth like a dog's, sometimes
> dancing on one bad leg!
> They do what they want, the dog's teeth say that.

The dancing rhythms still stagger, but as the speaker reflects on his ran-dom leaps, his stagger subsides:

> But I grew up without dog's teeth,
> showed a whole body,
> left only clear tracks in sand.
> I learned to walk swiftly, easily,
> no trace of a limp.
> I even leaped a little. Guess where my defect is!

His line "I even leaped" is practically a pun since his mind has been leaping wildly. He is nearing a point of insight. The next stanza asks, as if self-conscious of his previous limping rhythms:

> Then what? If a man, cautious,
> hides his limp,
> somebody has to limp it! Things
> do it; the surroundings limp.
> House walls get scars,
> the car breaks down; matter, in drudgery, takes it up.

A limp or a defect lives someplace. If it is not in me, it is in another, in a thing. At this breakthrough, his mind recreates his father's wedding, and the staggering of lines is associated with the character of his father. Here is the remainder of the poem:

> On my father's wedding day,
> no one was there
> to hold him. Noble loneliness
> held him. Since he never asked for pity
> his friends thought he
> was whole. Walking alone, he could carry it.
>
> He came in limping. It was a simple
> wedding, three
> or four people. The man in black,
> lifting the book, called for order.
> And the invisible bride
> stepped forward, before his own bride.
>
> He married the invisible bride, not his own.
> In her left
> breast she carried the three drops
> that wound and kill. He already had
> his bark-like skin then,
> made rough especially to repel the sympathy
>
> he longed for, didn't need, and wouldn't accept.
> So the Bible's
> words are read. The man in black

speaks the sentence. When the service
is over, I hold him
in my arms for the first time and the last.

After that he was alone
and I was alone.
Few friends came; he invited few.
His two-story house he turned
into a forest,
where both he and I are the hunters.

The son arrives imaginatively at his father's wedding because that ini-
tial log recalled his father in loneliness. The accumulated images draw him
inexorably to this moment: does his father do what he wants (the log image
returns in "bark-like skin"); does he limp, why? At the wedding itself, the
black-clothed man (who could be minister, undertaker, judge) reads the
"sentence" for the "service." These are frightening passages, intensely focused
on the scene—not leaping about—though in places moving swiftly. The
father's limp was in not wanting/needing/accepting sympathy; and his
divided image of his bride is equally a defect. Strangely, the son extends
sympathy: "I hold him / in my arms." The two maintain an estranged rela-
tionship of contraries in a split-level house, like a forest in which each seeks
for the other. The staggering rhythms are gone but the sounds of estrange-
ment are loud in the final image (house as forest) and line breaks:

His two-story house he turned
into a forest,
where both he and I are the hunters.

Notes

1. "An Interview with Ted Kooser," *Kenyon Review*, Winter, 2008

Chapter Six

Metaphor and Simile

We will move immediately to a poem by Seamus Heaney, the title poem from his book *Seeing Things,* for what we can learn about metaphor—*metaphor being a comparison of two unlike things*—and about the nature of seeing things with metaphoric eyes.

Seeing Things

I

Inishbofin on a Sunday morning.
Sunlight, turfsmoke, seagulls, boatslip, diesel.
One by one we were being handed down
Into a boat that dipped and shilly-shallied
Scaresomely every time. We sat tight
On short cross-benches, in nervous twos and threes,
Obedient, newly close, nobody speaking
Except the boatmen, as the gunwales sank
And seemed they might ship water any minute.
The sea was very calm but even so,
When the engine kicked and our ferryman
Swayed for balance, reaching for the tiller,
I panicked at the shiftiness and heft
Of the craft itself. What guaranteed us—
That quick response and buoyancy and swim—

Kept me in agony. All the time
As we went sailing evenly across
The deep, still, seeable-down-into water,
It was as if I looked from another boat
Sailing through air, far up, and could see
How riskily we fared into the morning,
And loved in vain our bare, bowed, numbered heads.

II

Claritas. The dry-eyed Latin word
Is perfect for the carved stone of the water
Where Jesus stands up to his unwet knees
And John the Baptist pours out more water
Over his head: all this in bright sunlight
On the façade of a cathedral. Lines
Hard and thin and sinuous represent
The flowing river. Down between the lines
Little antic fish are all go. Nothing else.
And yet in that utter visibility
The stone's alive with what's invisible:
Waterweed, stirred sand-grains hurrying off,
The shadowy, unshadowed stream itself.
All afternoon, heat wavered on the steps
And the air we stood up to our eyes in wavered
Like the zigzag hieroglyph for life itself.

III

Once upon a time my undrowned father
Walked into our yard. He had gone to spray
Potatoes in a field on the riverbank
And wouldn't bring me with him. The horse-sprayer
Was too big and newfangled, bluestone might
Burn me in the eyes, the horse was fresh, I
Might scare the horse, and so on. I threw stones
At a bird on the shed roof, as much for
The clatter of the stones as anything,
But when he came back, I was inside the house
And saw him out the window, scatter-eyed

And daunted, strange without his hat,
His step unguided, his ghosthood immanent.
When he was turning on the riverbank,
The horse had rusted and reared up and pitched
Cart and sprayer and everything off balance,
So the whole rig went over into a deep
Whirlpool, hoofs, chains, shafts, cartwheels, barrel
And tackle, all tumbling off the world,
And the hat already merrily swept along
The quieter reaches. That afternoon
I saw him face to face, he came to me
With his damp footprints out of the river,
And there was nothing between us there
That might not still be happily every after.

As the poem opens, Heaney's speaker is intent on specific things: "Sunlight, turfsmoke, seagulls, boatslip, diesel," as he sets out upon a risky sea ride. The scene is "Sunday morning" when in Irish Catholic culture one probably should be at church, not down with "boatslip, diesel." The dropping accents suggest a tension made plainer with "Scaresomely." While his language remains concrete—"handed down / Into a boat"—he is being gathered with his mates in a space remarkably church-like: "On short cross-benches, in nervous twos and threes, / Obedient, newly close, nobody speaking," waiting for the leader, the boatman. The leader becomes "the ferryman," like Charon bearing souls across the river Acheron, as if this were the journey to death.

The observed details subtly take on associated meanings as if metaphoric: the boat is a church. While he feels "in agony," he suddenly pulls back from direct observation of "The deep, still, seeable-down-into water" toward reconsideration: "as if I looked from another boat / Sailing through air." He is *seeing* several things, or rather he is *seeing a thing* in several ways, the object becoming something other.

A metaphor is a comparison of two unlike things, things that may not have been previously associated. Heaney's speaker perceives a floating, unstable boat as an airy craft. That is metaphor. Having made this connection, he nevertheless seems unable to sustain the power of seeing metaphorically, which would be a way of easing his terror. Even though the boat was "sailing evenly," he still feels vulnerable: "How riskily," "loved in vain our bare, bowed, numbered heads." It is as if he is uncertain not only of his metaphoric ability but of the capacity of things to be metaphoric, that is, to have a valid connection with something abstract: boat with airy craft. It may even be his faith that he doubts—"Sunday morning" suggests that—or that faith can exist. In this Christian world metaphoric thinking is normal: that is, one moves from seeing objects to "seeing" abstraction or spirit (for example: a church has a *nave*, from Latin *navis* for boat; a boat in an unsettled sea recalls Christ asleep in a storm-tossed boat). In Christian thought one moves from an object to the transcendental and to the sacramental: a sacrament is an action (e.g., baptizing) with an *object* (water) that *signifies* a spiritual event (receiving grace). So while the speaker employs metaphor, he simultaneously questions what metaphor can do, whether it is perhaps valid at all any more: when are things just things and when are they something else too? [1]

Part II of "Seeing Things" changes his approach: *Claritas* (clarity) is exactly what his anxiety prevented him from having aboard his craft. Here the stone of the cathedral, an actual thing, has both "visibility" and metaphoric power to reveal something else: "alive with what's invisible." The poem explicitly establishes comparisons: lines *represent* a flowing river, and the "air we stood in wavered / Like the zigzag hieroglyph for life itself"; a word carved on the facade of a cathedral suggests the meeting of Christ and John, and Christian meanings (symbols) like fish.

There is, besides, another level of metaphoric connection of unlike things: references to word and line and between-the-line meanings relate to poetry as well as to carved stone, poetry also being an unstable "craft."

In Part III, we are absorbed as in Part I with enumerated things.

> Once upon a time my undrowned father
> Walked into our yard. He had gone to spray
> Potatoes in a field on the riverbank
> And wouldn't bring me with him. The horse-sprayer
> Was too big and newfangled, bluestone might
> Burn me in the eyes, the horse was fresh, I
> Might scare the horse, and so on. I threw stones
> At a bird on the shed roof, as much for
> The clatter of the stones as anything,

The father's warning is of the danger of actual things: "Might scare the horse, and so on," much to the boy's annoyance.

Unlike in the first section where the speaker feels unsure about metaphoric connections, the boy clearly believes the concrete present. As the father returns from his near-drowning, the boy "sees" that "ghosthood" for his father is "immanent," that is, father can and will die. While it might appear that he sees in a vision his dead father, the boy in fact gains *insight* that death is to come, so that between him and his father there now is and will be "nothing between us."

Many words link parts of "Seeing Things": the "risk" of Part I is taken for granted by the father who accepts the dangers of farming; the meanings of water are central in Part II where standing in air is like standing in water reading the "hieroglyph of life"; by the end the fear of death (in Part I) is borne "happily ever after" by the boy.

Our emphasis so far has been on Heaney's speaker, the person in the poem who is talking about his experiences. But what about us: can we speak the poem to hear its metaphorical working? What would a metaphor sound like? How would we say it?

We know from our treatment of line and sound and rhythm and the like that we hear a poem's movement, that all elements of a poem's prosody reveal its meaning and emotion. As we listen to the opening lines of this poem, we can hear the way it prepares us for the presence of metaphor.

> Inishbofin on a Sunday morning.
> Sunlight, turfsmoke, seagulls, boatslip, diesel.
> One by one we were being handed down
> Into a boat that dipped and shilly-shallied
> Scaresomely every time.

The compound nouns seem assured: "sunlight, turfsmoke,... boatslip," but the voice drops on the final syllables: **MORN**-ing, **SUN**-light, **TURF**-smoke, **SEA**-gulls, **BOAT**-slip, **DIE**-sel, to create a drop in that assurance. Heaney prepares the movement of the poem with this sense of hesitance, but shortly the emotion changes to constraint:

> We sat tight
> On short cross-benches, in nervous twos and threes,
> Obedient, newly close, nobody speaking
> Except the boatmen, as the gunwales sank
> And seemed they might ship water any minute.

The sentence, and its language, feels enclosed, emphasis falling on "tight," on "twos and threes." Following further description of the action, he panics "in agony," but then appear three lines:

> All the time
> As we went sailing evenly across
> The deep, still, seeable-down-into water,

which, while smooth in expression, form an incomplete clause that anticipates change: the acute attention to the deep "seeable-down-into water." We hear changes in the man's perceptions just before his metaphorical insight:

> It was as if I looked from another boat
> Sailing through air, far up, . . .

We hear his movement from uncertainty to insight, to metaphor.

In the second stanza, we hear not an anxious voice-drop, but straight-forward statements (the keynote is *Claritas*) which move firmly to "cathedral." The metaphoric representation then appears:

> Lines
> Hard and thin and sinuous represent
> The flowing river.

Following this steady assertion, we hear the first vocal nervousness with "Little antic fish are all go," and then "Waterweed, stirred sand-grains hurrying off," and the final "zigzag hieroglyph for life." In these lines, we can hear the objects reach over to metaphoric linkages, where the "utter visibility" of stone is alive with "what's invisible."

In Part III, while we hear the drive of statemental, descriptive lines, we also encounter the boy's anger at not being allowed to accompany his father: "too big . . . newfangled, bluestone . . . Burn," "scare the horse, and so on. I threw stones." The father's near-disaster is anticipated in the "clatter" of the boy's tossed stone, before the real clatter of the upset wagon:

> the whole rig went over into a deep
> Whirlpool, hoofs, chains, shafts, cartwheels, barrel
> And tackle, all tumbling off the world,

In Part I, the catalogue's dropping accents suggested hesitance, but this list's compounds and one-syllable nouns run in a chaotic rush (many spondees). The change from pure description to insight begins:

> But when he came back, I was inside the house
> And saw him out the window, scatter-eyed
> And daunted, strange without his hat,
> His step unguided, his ghosthood immanent.

The surprised sounds of words like "scatter-eyed," "daunted," "strange," and finally "ghosthood" signal the boy's new vision of his father, not so much a formal metaphor itself as a sign of his metaphoric capability to see the un-real with "nothing between us." Throughout this poem, the lines, syntax, sounds, and emphases give voice to the metaphors we can indeed hear.

Basics of Metaphoric Thinking

Poetry is founded on metaphor: imagination conjoins separate things to enable poet and reader to see things in our world in a fresh, often pleasurable, and instructive way. Aristotle, as we saw in chapter one, was one of the first to say that metaphor is the heart of poetry. Centuries later, Robert Frost wrote, "Every poem is a new metaphor inside or it is nothing."

A real relationship is made through the energy of metaphor, a true creation, not just a "well, sort of like . . . ." That is why, once we experience a metaphor, we are changed by its insight and can scarcely see or hear that situation in the same fashion. We hear "Tyger Tyger burning bright / In the forests of the night," and the denseness of night can never be the same.

Metaphor explores feelings we may not understand or be able to put a name to (is Heaney's speaker afraid of the unstable boat or of something else?). It acts as a bridge between our feelings and natural things so that our interior feelings are identified in the exterior/concrete. For example, if someone we like suddenly becomes unfeeling and rejects our affection, we might say, "He's changed." But that conveys neither understanding nor the impact of the experience, and we need understanding as much as we need the power to express it. Almost instinctively, we have recourse to comparisons: "He felt a million miles away." "It felt as if a wall of rocks fell between us." "She just dried up, evaporated." Each of these figures strives toward a distinct emotion: distance, barrier, shock.

Effective metaphor tells or shows us something which cannot be paraphrased or simplified by direct statement. Here is one from George Mackay Brown's poem "Haddock Fishermen":

> Sunset drives a butcher blade
> In the day's throat.

This figure is harsh like the fishermen's work and expressive of an attitude beyond description of color alone.

In Langston Hughes' poem "Song for a Dark Girl," a young woman feels the death of her lynched lover:

> Love is a naked shadow
>   On a gnarled and naked tree.

Love compared to a shadow, the first metaphor, could lead in several directions, but the next line links it to a lynching. The tree itself is naked as if human, so "gnarled" is both the tree and by extension the distorted shadow. Her emotions are embedded in the harsh language of the metaphor.

Simile

Whereas in metaphor one thing *is* another, in *simile* one thing *is like* another. For example, if we say "my love *is* a red red rose," we are pointing to a full equivalence. But "my love is *like* a red red rose" selects only a few characteristics. Simile makes a partial linkage, not less meaningful but more confined than metaphor. Ordinarily, we hear the explicit turn of simile in its words "like" or "as" or "resemble."

In "The Scattered Congregation," Swedish poet Tomas Tranströmer (translation by Robert Bly) uses both metaphor and simile:

> 1
>
> We got ready and showed our home.
> The visitor thought: you live well.
> The slum must be inside you.
>
> 2
>
> Inside the church, pillars and vaulting
> white as plaster, like the cast
> around the broken arm of faith.

Tranströmer's images of home and of living well are clear enough to grasp. The shock of surprise comes with "slum": showing our home may be pleasurable, but the metaphorical "slum" as an aspect of our home is abrupt, if we consider a slum to be unpleasant. In the ideal, living well in our home ought to be harmonious with a healthy inner life, but the slum figure is pointedly placed "inside you." The external evidence of living "well" is contrasted with interior disrepair, insofar as "slum" suggests neglect, possibly moral slovenliness. The metaphor would run thus: If living well is not also the interior condition of your house, you are secreting a slum inside yourself. (The title "The Scattered Congregation" is paradoxical, for a congregation—literally, a flock of sheep—is by definition a unity.)

As the repetition of "inside" links church and slum, a simile links the church's pillars and vaulting, "white *as* plaster." With the next simile, "*like* the cast,*"* a broken limb is explicitly linked to faith; that is, both casts and faith are plastered over and whitened as if with pretense. Nowhere does the poem suggest that white plaster is anything but a covering on something unpleasant, for the similes isolate associations of whiteness to plaster and cast.

Following Simile in a Poem

Concerning poems—and everything else—there are things that we know, things that we do not know, and things we know that we may not realize we know. Usually with simile we understand both terms, but a poet may develop a figure in order to explore the comparison. Robert Hass's "Heroic Simile" explores what the comparative power of simile can mean to us. The heroic simile (also called Homeric and epic simile) is an extended comparison. For example, in the *Iliad*, in order to hear King Agamemnon, the people "swarmed like bees that sally from some hollow cave and flit in countless throng among the spring flowers, bunched in knots and clusters" (*Iliad*, Book II, translated by Robert Fagles). We may not know each of Hass's similes, or even that some are similes, but we will know at what point the power of simile-making fails, and what that means.

Heroic Simile

When the swordsman fell in Kurosawa's *Seven Samurai*
in the gray rain,

in Cinemascope and the Tokugawa dynasty,
he fell straight as a pine, he fell
as Ajax fell in Homer
in chanted dactyls and the tree was so huge
the woodsman returned for two days
to that lucky place before he was done with the sawing
and on the third day he brought his uncle.

They stacked logs in the resinous air,
hacking the small limbs off,
tying those bundles separately.
The slabs near the root
were quartered and still they were awkwardly large;
the logs from midtree they halved:
ten bundles and four great piles of fragrant wood,
moons and quarter moons and half moons
ridged by the saw's tooth.

The woodsman and the old man his uncle
are standing in midforest
on a floor of pine silt and spring mud.
They have stopped working
because they are tired and because
I have imagined no pack animal
or primitive wagon. They are too canny
to call in neighbors and come home
with a few logs after three days' work.
They are waiting for me to do something
or for the overseer of the Great Lord
to come and arrest them.

How patient they are!
The old man smokes a pipe and spits.
The young man is thinking he would be rich
if we were already rich and had a mule.
Ten days of hauling
and on the seventh day they'll probably
be caught, go home empty-handed

or worse. I don't know
whether they're Japanese or Mycenaean
and there's nothing I can do.
The path from here to that village
is not translated. A hero, dying,
gives off stillness to the air.
A man and a woman walk from the movies
to the house in the silence of separate fidelities.
There are limits to imagination.

The terms we need to know are Japanese film-maker Kurosawa (1954),
a panoramic film process (CinemaScope, 1953–67), eighteenth-century
Japanese samurai culture (Tokugawa), and the Greek epic culture of
Homer's *Iliad* and Ajax. Hass uses similes in his poem but at the same time
questions their uses, or rather asks what it means for us to employ simile as
a valid comparison. His similes develop in this fashion: *Seven Samurai* is a
film representation of (*like*) the Samurai warrior, who is *like* the Homeric
hero Ajax, and both are *like (as)* the hero that fell. The fallen pine is tower-
ing and majestic *as* a hero. Who comes to this stately tree but a woodsman
and his uncle, who are *not like* anyone else in the heroic tradition. They
are not intent on anything more meaningful than methodically cutting up
the tree. Heroic simile takes for granted an heroic ideal which establishes
a living relationship between the two terms, but the woodsman and his
uncle seem to have no ideal, no connection with heroes; they do not think
in similes nor chant in heroic dactyls. Thus, they are without tradition and
without motivation to work toward anything but the pragmatic end of a
woodpile.

We hear the sweaty labor of the woodsmen as they stack and hack, tie,
quarter, and halve the logs and slabs. The lines' sound is sharp and energetic
until "ridged by the saw's tooth," when we hear cessation of the woods-
men's action:

The woodsman and the old man his uncle
are standing in midforest
on a floor of pine silt and spring mud.
They have stopped working
because they are tired and because

The lines have lost energy. The wood is no longer "fragrant," the air no longer sweet with resin. The men stand, in mud, exhausted. The reason for this stasis is the absence of the motivating power of the heroic ideal. And this absence also infects the poet: dullness settles "because / I have imagined no pack animal / or primitive wagon." Imagination, the poet's power of simile, has stopped. As we listen to the movement of the poem, the impact of comparison—Ajax as hero, samurai as hero—lasts as long as the heroic image lasts. A simile being an imagined construct, the poet too stops, standing helpless in spring mud, unable to imagine. He admits to having lost the knowledge which a poet is supposed to have of Japanese and ancient Greek heroic traditions.

Three lines from the end, another person appears who has been conspicuously absent: a woman. She is not connected, as she would be by imagination or simile, to the man. Movies are representations of (*like*) the real. Kurosawa's film was a true simile-representation of the demise of the samurai hero (who dies in the gray rain). But these two walk in silence (no chants) from generic "movies" to "the" house. No simile or promise of connection is made. So long as imagination believes itself to be limited, there can only be "man," "woman."

"Heroic Simile" employs similes to illustrate the force of such thinking, just as its lack of similes signifies the demise of interconnectedness. A desperate poem, it illustrates the profound consequences both of similitic thinking and its collapse. It challenges our assumption of the possibility of literature, which is based, like all life in fact, on imagination and the validity of metaphoric and similitic associations. However, it is a poem, an imagined and created form, so possibility may still exist.

Note

1 Seeing things and seeing something *in* those things is what we call *double vision*. This is the way poet William Blake put it:

> For double the vision my eyes do see,
> And a double vision is always with me;
> With my inward eye 'tis an old man gray;
> With my outward a thistle across the way.

It is as if we have two sets of eyes: the optical pair that *sees* a thing and the inner pair that *makes* it something else, connecting natural to human. While objects retain value, we can transcend the merely objective. For example: we see a parent or child whom we love with different eyes than we see a random passerby. Love's "blindness" means we see in a loved one something quite different from a deposit of carbon and water. Conversely, in a world without imagination, sexual intimacy would be equally suitable with anybody; only imagination makes love meaningful.

We would find it almost impossible to live seeing things strictly literally. If we go to a shop to buy a blouse, any one that fits should be suitable. How the one we buy differs from others depends on our (double) view of it as fashionable or beautiful. We pick up two peaches that are essentially the same: we select one that "looks" good or "appears" ripe, juicy.

See also Northrop Frye, *Double Vision: Language and Meaning in Religion,* (Toronto: University of Toronto Press, 1991.)

Chapter Seven

Rhyme

Children rhyme their chants and skip-rope songs. School-day rhymes that assist in remembering Latin prepositions may lodge forever in our minds. Rhyme can bring music to words with its chiming sound. It can, if very obvious, become comical or satiric. When encompassing many words, as in contemporary rap, rhyme can celebrate one's ingenuity and spontaneity with language. In fact, the pervasiveness of hip-hop and rap in contemporary culture has stimulated young poets toward employing rhyme again. It has been, of course, fixed fast in the tradition of English verse, as it is in the verse of many languages, some far more complex than any English writers could duplicate, such as ancient Welsh.

When we speak of rhyme, we usually mean words sounding alike, a repetition of sounds: pin–thin, stink–rink, June–tune–croon–spoon . . . , or polysyllabic rhymes: visit–is it, master–disaster. But making words or syllables sound alike does not account for all the ways poets make sounds connect with one another.

We will start with a principle that rhyme works as a binding force in poems, connecting words, lines, and stanzas in various patterns, sometimes obvious, sometimes quiet, until we enunciate and release the echoes. Rhyme is used from the amusing to the darkest and soberest of moods. The presence of rhyme is itself no guarantee of specific emotion or tone, any more than a fixed metrical pattern is. What matters is that we hear in the rhymes the way they function in each poem.

Exact and Varied Rhyme

We usually think of rhyme occurring at line ends, as in Alexander Pope's famous couplet,

> A little learning is a dangerous thing;
> Drink deep, or taste not the Pierian spring.
> (*An Essay on Criticism*, 1711)

We may also think of rhyme as exact in sound. But since pronunciations differ and change over time, over nations, over communities, exact sound may not be possible. English—most languages for that matter—will sound very different across a matter of miles (various dialects), let alone across continents. In *The Rape of the Lock*, Pope's exact rhyme of "obey–tea" (**TAY** not **TEE**) may sound a bit odd to American ears but it was normal pronunciation to him. (We will return to the issue of exact rhyme.)

Pope's couplet about learning is called a closed or heroic couplet, which means that each pair of ten-syllable lines rhymes and tends to end-stop. The rhyming thus closes and binds the pair into a succinct and memorable observation, as if it could stand by itself.

When rhyme becomes obvious, we may think it is frivolous or, in this capital example, plain hilarious. Huck Finn, being exposed for the first time to "Poetry," tries to be impressed but cannot quite bring himself to lie about it:

> *Ode to Stephen Dowling Bots, Dec'd.*
>
> And did young Stephen sicken,
>   And did young Stephen die?
> And did sad hearts thicken
>   And did the mourners cry?
>
> No; such was not the fate of
>   Young Stephen Dowling Bots;
> Though sad hearts round him thickened,
>   'Twas not from sickness' shots.
>
> No whooping-cough did rack his frame,
>   Nor measles drear, with spots;
> Not these impaired the sacred name
>   Of Stephen Dowling Bots.

Young Emmeline Grangerford's rhymes (*Huckleberry Finn*, chapter XVII) are so predictable that any group of listeners can unerringly shout out the rhyme words. And like Huck, we may not be able to keep a straight face. This predictability occurs because the weight of meaning falls regularly on each rhyme word—"sicken–die–thicken–cry"—so we anticipate its being stressed (except for "fate of–thickened"). If this kind of rhyming sounds like doggerel, how does a poet avoid such a fate? A skilled practitioner of the couplet is able to skirt the hazard of too obvious rhyme. Back to Pope:

> This nymph, to the destruction of mankind,
> Nourish'd two locks, which graceful hung behind
> In equal curls, and well conspir'd to deck
> With shining ringlets the smooth iv'ry neck.
> (The Rape of the Lock, II, 19–22)

Because the sentence is constructed thus—"Nymph, nourished, locks that hung and conspired to deck"—emphasis draws away from the ring of rhyme and falls on these main words. Enjambed lines also redirect stress from line-end to line-beginning: "behind / In equal curls." The same shifting to the key object occurs in "to deck / With shining ringlets."

The Effects of Rhyme

The repeated sounds of rhyme do more than simply sound pleasant. Rhyme promotes unity, and this unifying impulse can become thematic. Pope's well regulated verse supported his belief that order is essential to artistic and social life. We explored in Denise Levertov's "Stepping Westward" (under "Line," chapter one) how her two-line grouping (rarely rhymed) parallels her pairing with her husband and the dual tensions she feels, whether she is two or one.

English poetry's most common rhyming pattern may well be the ABAB quatrain. It is an effective scheme because, although the rhyme words are separated, they shape the stanza. Wordsworth employs ABAB frequently (the poem's title is first line):

> Strange fits of passion have I known:
> And I will dare to tell,
> But in the Lover's ear alone,
> What once to me befell.

When she I loved looked every day
Fresh as a rose in June,
I to her cottage bent my way,
Beneath an evening-moon.

Upon the moon I fixed my eye,
All over the wide lea;
With quickening pace my horse drew nigh
Those paths so dear to me.

And now we reached the orchard-plot;
And, as we climbed the hill,
The sinking moon to Lucy's cot
Came near, and nearer still.

In one of those sweet dreams I slept,
Kind Nature's gentlest boon!
And all the while my eyes I kept
On the descending moon.

My horse moved on; hoof after hoof
He raised, and never stopped:
When down behind the cottage roof,
At once, the bright moon dropped.

What fond and wayward thoughts will slide
Into a Lover's head!
"O mercy!" to myself I cried,
"If Lucy should be dead!"

Wordsworth controls and varies his rhyme to suggest first the lover's anticipation in the high "i" sounds of stanza three, which then drop in the next to "o" sounds that inspire suspense of dire expectation. The first line end-stops so what follows is a narration of his story. Stanza two unifies "Fresh" and "I"—neither are rhyme words—and the words "evening-moon" modify the rhyming with "June." But as the speaker advances on his careful horse and reaches his goal, the pathos has so increased that when we hear "Lover's head" we know the rhyme will be "dead." Wordsworth stresses the rhymes of these words to drive home the tragedy both we and the lover expect.

This ABAB form is, of course, adaptable to other emotions, for example, Anthony Hecht's amusing "'It Out-Herods Herod. Pray you, Avoid it.'" Hecht's stressed rhymes evoke a slangy humor, yet they can still surprise: "hunch" does not presume "punch."

> Tonight my children hunch
> Toward their Western, and are glad
> As, with a Sunday punch,
> The Good casts out the Bad.
>
> And in their fairy tales
> The warty giant and witch
> Get sealed in doorless jails
> And the match-girl strikes it rich.
>
> I've made myself a drink.
> The giant and witch are set
> To bust out of the clink
> When my children have gone to bed.
>
> All frequencies are loud
> With signals of despair;
> In flash and morse they crowd
> The rondure of the air.
>
> For the wicked have grown strong,
> Their numbers mock at death,
> Their cow brings forth its young,
> Their bull engendereth.
>
> Their very fund of strength,
> Satan, bestrides the globe;
> He stalks its breadth and length
> And finds out even Job.
>
> Yet by quite other laws
> My children make their case;
> Half God, half Santa Claus,
> But with my voice and face,

A hero comes to save
The poorman, beggarman, thief,
And make the world behave
And put an end to grief.

And that their sleep be sound
I say this childermas
Who could not, at one time,
Have saved them from the gas.

The rhymes continue to jar—"death," "engendereth," "childermas," "gas"—as the poem shakes itself from humor toward somber reflections on the lives of his children and his own possibly helpless fatherhood.

Internal Rhymes

While rhymes often fall at line-ends, they can as well appear inside lines. Wordsworth repeated "moon" and rhymed it with "hoof" and "roof." In "The Rime of the Ancient Mariner," Coleridge utilized the oral, storytelling power of the ballad with its formulaic phrasing which often involves repeating sounds:

He holds him with his glittering eye—
The Wedding-Guest stood still,
And listens like a three years' child:
The Mariner hath his will.

Internal vowels are rhymed, for example: "him," "his," glittering," "still, "listens," and "will." In other places, Coleridge rhymed words and syllables within lines:

At length did cross an Albatross; . . .

The ice did split with a thunder-fit; . . .

In mist or cloud, on mast or shroud.

(In the last line, "mist–mast" are near-rhymes.) The intensity of the end and internal rhymes seems to be part of the old mariner's strategy to mesmerize his auditor and hold him fast with magically close sound effects.

Tennyson rhymed intensely in "The Lady of Shalott" (not all are marked):

> On either side the river lie
> Long fields of barley and of rye,
> That clothe the wold and meet the sky;
> And through the field the road runs by
>   To many-towered Camelot;
> And up and down the people go,
> Gazing where the lilies blow
> Round an island there below,
>   The island of Shalott. (Part I)

The sudden lack of rhyme in "To many-towered Camelot" is striking. After four more lines, we hear the beginning of a rhyming refrain that extends across larger groups of lines: Camelot–Shalott. Such internal rhymes consist of either repeated vowel sounds, called *assonance,* or repeated consonant sounds, called *alliteration.*

The effect of Lord Byron's rhymes in *Don Juan* is quite different (he later rhymes "Juan" with "new one" and "true one"):

> Young Juan now was sixteen years of age,
>   Tall, handsome, slender, but well knit; he seemed
> Active, though not so sprightly, as a page;
>   And everybody but his mother deemed
> Him almost a man; but she flew in a rage
>   And bit her lips (for else she might have screamed)
> If any said so, for to be precocious
> Was in her eyes a thing the most atrocious.
>   (*Don Juan*, Canto I, 54)

Byron's ABABABCC rhymes become comical by his nonchalant and partly parenthetical phrasing—"And bit her lips (for else she might have screamed)," as if to force a rhyme as he does with three-syllable rhymes.

Rhyme and Tone

One way to see and hear the divergent ways a similar rhyme scheme can be used is with two poems by William Blake, the first from *Songs of Innocence,* the second from *Songs of Experience*. They are both rhymed ABCB, yet being from different books, they diverge sharply in emotional tone and act as contraries to each other.

Nurse's Song

When the voices of children are heard on the green
And laughing is heard on the hill,
My heart is at rest within my breast
And every thing else is still.

Then come home my children, the sun is gone down
And the dews of night arise;
Come come leave off play, and let us away
Till the morning appears in the skies.

No no let us play, for it is yet day
And we cannot go to sleep;
Besides in the sky, the little birds fly
And the hills are all cover'd with sheep.

Well well go & play till the light fades away
And then go home to bed.
The little ones leaped & shouted & laughed
And all the hills echoèd.

Nurse's Song

When the voices of children are heard on the green
And whisprings are in the dale:
The days of my youth rise fresh in my mind,
My face turns green and pale.

Then come home my children, the sun is gone down
And the dews of night arise;
Your spring & your day are wasted in play
And your winter and night in disguise.

Such a rhyme pattern moderates close sound effects, and the long lines also delay the return of rhyme so we attend more to what is being described than to the muted music. There is, however, a consistent internal consonantal rhyme like child**REN**–gre**EN**, and syllable rhyme—"rest–breast." What changes in the *Experience* poem are sound effects and diction: "Laughing" has turned to ominous "whisperings." The internal echoes of "dale–days–face" and of "green–green" offer not harmonies but ironies, because the rigid nurse is filled with bitter memories ("green and pale"), and claims childish games are wasteful, and what rises are unhealthy "dews."

The rhymes of A. E. Housman seem masked in simplicity, almost triviality. From *Last Poems*, number 23:

> In the morning, in the morning,
>> In the happy field of hay,
> Oh they looked at one another
>> By the light of day.
>
> In the blue and silver morning
>> On the haycock as they lay,
> Oh they looked at one another
>> And they looked away.

What begins with happy fields, "the blue and silver morning," and lilting promise of a pastoral idyll, turns to hard rejection. While the ABCB ABCB pattern seems to harmonize the scene, the truncated rhythm of the fourth line so confuses the rhyme that much music is lost.

From Housman's same collection, number 32,

> When I would muse in boyhood
>> The wild green woods among,
> And nurse resolves and fancies
>> Because the world was young,
> It was not foes to conquer,
>> Nor sweethearts to be kind,
> But it was friends to die for
>> That I would seek and find.
>
> I sought them far and found them,
>> The sure, the straight, the brave,
> The hearts I lost my own to,
>> The souls I could not save.

> They braced their belts about them,
> > They crossed in ships the sea,
> They sought and found six feet of ground,
> > And there they died for me.

The syntax often seems skewed as if to force rhymes: "The wild green woods among," "They crossed in ships the sea," and only two pairs of lines in each stanza rhyme, in a complex, perhaps disturbing, pattern. Accompanying these tensions is the disillusion that lurks in the "When" of boyhood musing, in the too-perfect green woods, in the speaker's longing for meaningful death. The second stanza turns frankly more bleak. When the war imagery of belts and ships appears, he reflects on those fine youth, knowing now whence they are bound. The final two lines ("six feet" echoing the sounds of "ships the sea") draw the tragic reversal of his boys' hopes: "they died for me."

The same dislocation of rhyme's potential harmony occurs in T. S. Eliot's "Love Song of J. Alfred Prufrock":

> Let us go then, you and I,
> When the evening is spread out against the sky
> Like a patient etherised upon a table;

We feel a considerable shock when the two pretty rhyming lines abruptly stop. But while the failure of expected rhyme can be devastating, continued rhymes may contrast against a poem's more dreadful meaning and sour the music of repeated sounds. The close rhymes seem mocking:

> Streets that follow like a tedious argument
> Of insidious intent
> To lead you to an overwhelming question. . . .
> Oh, do not ask, "What is it?"
> Let us go and make our visit.
>
> > In the room the women come and go
> Talking of Michaelangelo.

Off-Rhymes

Some rhymes sound inexact, a little wrong. Such rhymes are far too common to be accidents or failures. We call these by various names: off-rhymes, slant-rhymes, or eye-rhymes (similar spelling, different pronunciation). Any of these may disturb the harmony of exact rhyme, giving us a linkage but not the assurance of perfectly fitted rhymes. There is no nice rule here, but it is reasonable to assume that an inexact rhyme may call attention to a degree of tension and disruption in meaning.

Geoffrey Hill frequently off-rhymes, here in "Ovid in the Third Reich" (Ovid, the Latin poet of the *Metamorphoses*):

> I love my work and my children. God
> Is distant, difficult. Things happen.
> Too near the ancient troughs of blood
> Innocence is no earthly weapon.
>
> I have learned one thing: not to look down
> So much upon the damned. They, in their sphere,
> Harmonize strangely with the divine
> Love. I, in mine, celebrate the love-choir.

The striking line breaks help to dislocate the rhymes, as if the coherence of true rhyme would be absurd to this speaker. The off-rhyming in "God–blood" and "happen–weapon" both link and separate each pair. In the second stanza, the consonantal rhyming of "down–divine" and "sphere–choir" creates more strange harmony.

The WWI poet Wilfred Owen used off-rhymes to reject any union between music and the violence of battle. Here is "Arms and the Boy":

> Let the boy try along this bayonet-blade
> How cold steel is, and keen with hunger of blood;
> Blue with all malice, like a madman's flash;
> And thinly drawn with famishing for flesh.
>
> Lend him to stroke these blind, blunt bullet-heads
> Which long to nuzzle in the hearts of lads.
> Or give him cartridges of fine zinc teeth,
> Sharp with the sharpness of grief and death.
>
> For his teeth seem for laughing round an apple.
> There lurk no claws behind his fingers supple;
> And God will grow no talons at his heels,
> Not antlers through the thickness of his curls.

With "blade–blood," "flash–flesh," "leads–lads," "teeth–death" we hear the grinding paradox of off-rhyming words, for to Owen the weaponry is eager to chew up boys' bodies. Internally, "steel" rhymes with "keen" just as "steel is" rhymes with "malice." In his poem "Dulce et Decorum Est," Owen true-rhymes "glory" with "mori," the Latin word "to die," so that the entire sense of the poem is distilled in those two conflicting words.

In Yeats's "The Lake Isle of Innisfree," we hear a wonderful music of vowel sounds which are a pleasure to speak aloud:

> I will arise and go now, and go to Innisfree,
> And a small cabin build there, of clay and wattles made:
> Nine bean-rows will I have there, a hive for the honey-bee,
> And live alone in the bee-loud glade.

The emphatic "i" sounds of the opening half-line return in the third to create a beautiful sound as well as a thematic emphasis that this is the splendid world where I wish to dwell. No less joyous are the soothing "l" sounds (alliteration). While the long lines lull the dominance of rhyme, the sounds still repeat easily in the ear. Yeats's management of sound is masterly, his word repetitions thoughtful and warm. Before we go on, here is the rest of "The Lake Isle of Innisfree":

> And I shall have some peace there, for peace comes dropping slow,
> Dropping from the veils of the morning to where the cricket sings;
> There midnight's all a glimmer, and noon a purple glow,
> And evening full of the linnet's wings.
>
> I will arise and go now, for always night and day
> I hear lake water lapping with low sounds by the shore;
> While I stand on the roadway, or on the pavements grey,
> I hear it in the deep heart's core.

Other effects can be achieved by repeated vowel sounds. In a short passage from Whitman's "Out of the Cradle Endlessly Rocking," the tying "i" sounds develop an important thematic element:

> Yes my brother I know,
> The rest might not, but I have treasur'd every note,
> For more than once dimly down to the beach gliding,
> Silent, avoiding the moonbeams, blending myself with the shadows,

Recalling now the obscure shapes, the echoes, the sounds and
sights after their sorts,
The white arms out in the breakers tirelessly tossing,
I, with bare feet, a child, the wind wafting my hair,
Listen'd long and long.

While we hear the assonance—"I," "gliding, / Silent," "my-," "sights," "white,"
"tire-," "I," "child"—and the alliteration—"Listen'd loud and long"—the
repeated "I" drives the poem with a joyous personal exultation of what he
is doing.

However, the repeated "I" in the final stanzas of Robert Frost's "The
Road Not Taken" has an entirely opposite effect; by repeating "I" three
times and repeating the sound in the rhyme words, we hear an egocentric
stress on the old boy himself, as if he is trying to remake the past into a
meaningful lesson . . . for graduating seniors.

The Range of Rhyme: An Analysis

As we said to begin this chapter, what matters is that we both hear rhymes
and how they function in each poem. We will examine rhyme in contem-
porary poet John Logan's "Three Moves":

Three Moves

Three moves in six months and I remain
the same.
Two homes made two friends.
The third leaves me with myself again.
(We hardly speak.)
Here I am with tame ducks
and my neighbors' boats,
only this electric heat
against the April damp.
I have a friend named Frank—
The only one who ever dares to call
and ask me, "How's your soul?"
I hadn't thought about it for a while,
and was ashamed to say I didn't know.

I have no priest for now.
Who
will forgive me then. Will you?
Tame birds and my neighbors' boats.
The ducks honk about the floats ...
They walk dead drunk onto the land and grounds,
iridescent blue and black and green and brown.
They live on swill
our aged houseboats spill.
But still they are beautiful.
Look! The duck with its unlikely beak
has stopped to pick
and pull
at the potted daffodil.
Then again they sway home
to dream
bright gardens of fish in the early night.
Oh these ducks are all right.
They will survive.
But I am sorry I do not often see them climb.
Poor sons-a-bitching ducks.
You're all fucked up.
What do you do that for?
Why don't you hover near the sun anymore?
Afraid you'll melt?
These foolish ducks lack a sense of guilt,
and so all their multi-thousand-mile range
is too short for the hope of change.

Here is no soaring eagle, no necklaced albatross, no ravishing lark song, or even glowering raven. Just a duck. Or a flock of ducks. How serious can this poem be anyway?

Enjoying the delicious fun of Logan's rhyming is practically reward enough. He insists on connecting when connections seem impossible or weird. His rhymes connect persons and connect ducks, they isolate and join, they toy with everything, yet also match "melt" to "guilt" which are serious words in those final long lines, just as is the solid rhyme of "range–change."

Logan begins rhyming "remain–same" and "again," each word repeating his theme: things change but really do not. After these rhymes, what follows is less direct: "soul" rings (discordantly?) with "know–now." One of Logan's more daring uses of line and rhyme is

> Who
> will forgive me then. Will you?

"Tame" echoes "ashamed." Even "honk" sounds like "drunk." In those lines (18–19), we find clear couplet rhymes: "boats–floats," "grounds–brown," and the rhyme:

> They live on swill
> our aged houseboats spill.
> But still they are beautiful.

Is that last word pronounced "beauty-fil"? But then it would not rhyme with "pull," though there is still its lurking rhyme with "daffo-dil." By this time, we are attuned to accept any sound link, so why not "beak–pick"? The assonance of "night–right" continues in "survive–climb." Finally comes what we have half expected all along: what rhymes with duck? Yet in spite of that joke, these are not ducks to be scorned. They are—or at least used to be—mythic, for they soar(ed) to the sun like Icarus; they fly (flew) thousands of miles. And where do they leave me? With little change. Maybe hope.

With Logan, rhyme is funny/serious; it creates implausible harmonies; it can stretch sound-links (do "damp–Frank" rhyme, or "call–soul"?); it can reach across eight lines: "mile" echoes "climb." But his humor, of course, can have its rueful edge: "home" links with "dream."

Chapter Eight

Form

While we often think of forms of verse as intellectual and visible constructions, associated with the page, one can in fact hear form. That is, if one can hear line breaks and stanza breaks, can hear the grouping of couplets, quatrains, and sestets as well as larger complex structures, then we do indeed hear form.

All poems have form. Form can be either set and regulated, or invented. We see on a page the look or shape of a set form. A sonnet, for instance, has recognizable dimensions. A haiku has particular requirements of lines and syllables that we see at once. There is a ballad form, there is an epic form. Such visual appearances are *external form*. The *internal form*, then, is the intellectual and emotional force that moves through a poem and holds it together as an experience. Form means both a poem's outward shape and its inner harmony. What we hear as we speak or listen to a poem is the process of fulfillment of both kinds of form.

Though not stated in so many words, this book has been engaged, chapter by chapter, in matters of form. Line is form, for a poem is made of a series of lines which articulates the movement of the verse and creates the rhythmic pattern of the poem. Groups of lines or stanzas are also form, gradations or steps through which the poem proceeds to its culmination. Since the sounds of words in a line and through lines reveal meaning and emotion, sound creates a structure that can also be called form. Rhythm as form? No question. Rhythm inscribes the distinctive signature of the voice of the speaker, how it rises and falls, hastens and slows, hesitates, falls silent . . . until it ends. And of course there is metaphor, the imaginative structure and soul of a poem.

All elements of prosody are involved in making a poem into a distinct thing and giving it its shape that is both external and internal. A black bear and a brown bear and a grizzly bear might seem to have the same external shape. But were one to see a bear-like shape on a pathway at the edge of a forest, it would be prudent—i.e., essential to life and limb—to know that the disposition or inner form of each bear differs. One bear would run off, another would run us off. Many poems are written about the same topic, such as poems that "invite" a prospective lover to prove "all the pleasures" of love. But the individual emotion and meaning of each, the inner form, is distinct.

George Herbert's "The Church-floor" (discussed in chapter one) has both the visible form we see upon the page and the form or process of its intellectual and emotional development. Our discussion of that poem's use of line and the change and progress of the stanzas can be understood as being about its form. The form of William Carlos Williams's "To a Poor Old Woman" (also discussed in chapter one) is the visible shape on the page as well as the movement of the speaker's perception of the woman eating plums. Not, certainly, based on a pre-set structure of line and stanza, its form is invented as a way of expressing the speaker's perceptions of the old woman. It is this internal form or process that we hear. Each line is a meditation; the line breaks ensure a slow pace, and since each stanza is the next step in his perception, the stanza breaks too create audial hesitations. Through the careful vocal phrasing in what are recognizably American speech patterns—speech often is poetry—we anticipate each next detail, often changed by the line break to emphasize something different: "good to her," "good / to her," "taste / good to her." At the final stanza, we hear how she is "comforted," the plums a "solace," and the final line evokes her contentment.

> *To a Poor Old Woman*
>
> munching a plum on
> the street a paper bag
> of them in her hand
>
> They taste good to her
> They taste good

to her. They taste
good to her

You can see it by
the way she gives herself
to the one half
sucked out in her hand

Comforted
a solace of ripe plums
seeming to fill the air
They taste good to her

Form is often called *organic* when its shape grows out of the require-
ments or needs of its own progress (as an oak grows out of its acorn), dis-
covered or invented by the poet during composition. The internal form
thus operates by its own logic, appropriate to the speaker's perception.
Robert Bly's "My Father's Wedding" (chapter five) has a distinct internal
form which we can hear develop. Just as while listening to a sonata or a sym-
phony, we recognize each section beginning and ending, so when we listen
to a poem, the ear catches the movement from part to part, as line breaks,
stanza breaks, alterations of meter, of rhyme, and the like reveal changes.

Fixed Form Poems

The *sonnet*, a continuously popular and powerful form, is a conventional
poem, *convention* meaning a structure, device, or pattern that occurs regu-
larly in an art form. We look at a sonnet and recognize its formal require-
ments: fourteen lines with a customary division and distinct pattern of
rhyme.

The sonnet, like any fixed-form poem, comes out of an historical
demand for a verse that addresses a concern. The sonnet raised its head in
thirteen-century Sicily (not fully formed all at once, of course). At the heart
of the form lies this rationale: a concern, doubt, or tension is set forth and
then resolved. Because the intellectual or emotional issue is often a sizeable
one, the sonnet devotes the larger section, eight lines, to this exposition,
then discovers the solution in the final six lines. In the traditional rhyme
scheme of this compact form the eight lines are rhymed in two sets of four,

and the six lines are rhymed in two sets of three, or four and two. Given this traditional structure, the ear can usually follow the form of a sonnet.

In the English language the sonnet has two main versions, English and Italian. Perhaps the better known is the English or Shakespearean sonnet (composed by others before him too), written four-four-four-two, the conclusion held in a final couplet.

> That time of year thou mayst in me behold
> When yellow leaves, or none, or few, do hang
> Upon those boughs which shake against the cold,
> Bare ruined choirs, where late the sweet birds sang.
> In me thou see'st the twilight of such day
> As after sunset fadeth in the west,
> Which by and by black night doth take away,
> Death's second self that seals up all in rest.
> In me thou see'st the glowing of such fire
> That on the ashes of his youth doth lie,
> As the death-bed whereon it must expire,
> Consumed with that which it was nourished by.
>> This thou perceiv'st, which makes thy love more strong,
>> To love that well which thou must leave ere long.

Shakespeare's Sonnet 73 is a model of the form. Each quatrain ends with a period, and each has its own rhyme pattern, ABAB, CDCD, EFEF. Each quatrain expresses a separate image, and each image leads to the next until the solution is neatly enclosed in a rhymed pair, GG. Although this four-four-four-two pattern seems contrary to the basic eight-and-six format, it essentially is an eight-and-six sonnet. The third quatrain changes the image from darkness ("bare choirs," "black night") to "the glowing of such fire," a transition that signals the affirmation which will be completed in the couplet.

While the separately rhymed quatrains may suggest a difficulty in our hearing the sonnet's form, the repetitions of "in me" offer distinct clues to the movement, for each emphasizes another step forward. The sounds of the rhyming words contribute to the speaker's calm, until the couplet announces closure, not with "in me" but "This thou perceiv'st."

The Italian sonnet in English structures its initial eight in two sets of four and concludes with two sets of three. The octet is harmoniously rhymed ABBA ABBA, the sestet CDE CDE, for example, Milton's "When I Consider."

> When I consider how my light is spent,
> E'er half my days, in this dark world and wide,
> And that one talent which is death to hide,
> Lodg'd in me useless, though my soul more bent
> To serve therewith my Maker, and present
> My true account, lest he returning chide;
> "Doth God exact day-labor, light denied,"
> I fondly ask; But Patience to prevent
> That murmur, soon replies, "God does not need
> Either man's work or his own gifts; who best
> Bear his mild yoke, they serve him best; his state
> Is Kingly. Thousands at his bidding speed
> And post o'er land and ocean without rest:
> They also serve who only stand and wait."

In our discussion of this poem under "Pause" (chapter three) much is relevant to hearing its form:

> The first line advances steadily like his mind's search. At the near-parenthetical "in this dark world and wide," pauses enclose the phrase. Each subsequent pause has it own distinct duration and quality as the speaker is increasingly distracted:
>
> > Lodg'd in me useless, though my soul more bent
> > To serve therewith my Maker, and present
> > My true account, lest he returning chide;
> > "Doth God exact day-labor, light denied,"
> > I fondly ask. But Patience to prevent . . .
>
> A slight separation occurs between "Patience" and "to prevent" as she prepares her reply. The concluding two lines of the poem move steadfastly with a beautiful rising pitch on "stand and wait."

With no end-stop for each quatrain (though linked by rhyme), the sentence drives ahead until the midline break at line 8, after which the lines almost all enjamb until "rest." Hearing the emotional tensions throughout, we are relieved to be told that patience also has value.

Essentially, the Italian form has an eight-and-six format like the English but the parts differ in rhyme and thus in relation to one another; the concluding English couplet is also abandoned, and Milton holds his conclusion to the very last line: "They also serve who only stand and wait."

While accepting the conventions of the sonnet, poets are free to develop, stretch, or revise the form (usually still identifiable) in order to ring fresh meanings. A poet may, for example, conclude a sonnet with uncertainty and not resolution, and could even telescope the English (4, 4, 4, 2) and Italian (4, 4, 3, 3) forms. This Thomas Gray does in his mid-eighteenth century "Sonnet on the Death of Richard West":

> In vain to me the smiling mornings shine,
> And reddening Phoebus lifts his golden fire:
> The birds in vain their amorous descant join,
> Or cheerful fields resume their green attire:
> These ears, alas! for other notes repine,
> A different object do these eyes require.
> My lonely anguish melts no heart but mine;
> And in my breast the imperfect joys expire.
> Yet morning smiles the busy race to cheer,
> And new-born pleasure brings to happier men:
> The fields to all their wonted tribute bear;
> To warm their little loves the birds complain.
> I fruitless mourn to him that cannot hear,
> And weep the more because I weep in vain.

The poem seems to follow recognizable patterns. The four-line groups are set off by punctuation, a period ending line eight. The sestet promises resolution of the unhappiness with "Yet," and the period at line twelve prepares for a couplet conclusion (English). But the ABAB ABAB, CDC DCD rhyme (Italian) makes a couplet impossible. Further, the final lines offer unresolved sorrow, which we hear in the pained sounds of "complain," "vain," and the low "mourn," "more." We end as we began: "in vain." By violating the resolution which a sonnet promises, Gray increases the intensity of his isolation.

Elizabeth Bishop's "Sonnet (1979)" illustrates the changes one may ring and still call fourteen lines a sonnet. She inverts the eight-six form by ending two three-line groups with a period. The final two three-line groups end with an unrhymed pair. The lines are certainly not ten syllables, and the rhymes, such as "bubble–level," "divided–undecided," "away–gay," "level–bevel," are not in a preset pattern. Yet "Sonnet (1979)" literally depicts the "creature divided": it thematically divides-enjambs the form into six and eight—"Caught // Freed"—and thus retains the sonnet's pattern of tension and resolution, which for Bishop seems to be the essence of sonnet form.

> Caught—the bubble
> in the spirit level,
> a creature divided;
> and the compass needle
> wobbling and wavering,
> undecided.
> Freed—the broken
> thermometer's mercury
> running away;
> and the rainbow-bird
> from the narrow bevel
> of the empty mirror,
> flying wherever
> it feels like, gay!

In the short lines we hear the (partial) rhymes, but their brevity removes any certainty of anticipated form. The shift from "Caught" to "Freed" marks the turn of the sonnet form; the images too change from mechanical ("level," "compass") to natural and airy, "bird," "flying," until the uplifting concluding "gay" marks the end.

In each of these sonnet forms, the eight-and-six structure and the varied rhyme schemes allow us to hear development and resolution. The sonnet's brevity and consistency of form are especially responsive to the ear, for even when there is a marked divergence, the form retains its distinct audial development.

Sestina

Other fixed forms may be even more tightly regulated, longer, and more complex than the sonnet, yet still have a discernible audial form. In the *sestina*, a thirty-nine line poem, each six-line stanza is unrhymed but each end-word is repeated in succeeding stanzas: ABCDEF, FAEBDC, CFDABE, E . . . and so on, until the three lines of the seventh and final stanza (called the envoy) include all rhyme words.

When Alberto Rios wrote his sestina called "Nani," he felt free to refigure it as suited his needs:

Sitting at her table, she serves
the sopa de arroz to me
instinctively, and I watch her;
the absolute mama, and eat words
I might have had to say more
out of embarrassment. To speak,
now-foreign words I used to speak,
too, dribble down her mouth as she serves
me albondigas. No more
than a third are easy to me.
By the stove she does something with words
and looks at me only with her
back. I am full. I tell her
I taste the mint, and watch her speak
smiles at the stove. All my words
make her smile. Nani never serves
herself, she only watches me
with her skin, her hair. I ask for more.

I watch the mama warming more
tortillas for me. I watch her
fingers in the flame for me.
Near her mouth, I see a wrinkle speak
of a man whose body serves
the ants like she serves me, then more words
from more wrinkles about children, words
about this and that, flowing more
easily from those other mouths. Each serves
as a tremendous string around her,
holding her together. They speak
nani was this and that to me
and I wonder just how much of me
will die with her, what were the words

I could have been, was. Her insides speak
through a hundred wrinkles, now, more
than she can bear, steel around her,
shouting, then, What is this thing she serves?

She asks me if I want more.
I own no words to stop her.
Even before I speak, she serves.

Against the sestina's customary use of six stanzas and a three-line envoy, Rios makes two 18-line stanzas before the separated envoy (still 39 lines). While the rhyming is complex, the predominant word "serves" repeats in lines 1, 8 and 16, four more times in stanza two, and as the last word of the poem. The line-end words "me–her–words–more–speak," which are repeated in various patterns, create a distinct audial pattern that flows into the powerfully moving distillation of the envoy. As we hear the words return in such close pattern, we hear the true import of "nani" for the speaker, his emotion and esteem for the one who serves. That is what the sestina does: its reiterated words and patterns *make* meaning: the repetition inexorably increases and deepens his emotion for "nani."

Villanelle

Originally a folk song or pastoral poem, the *villanelle* consists of five three-line stanzas of equal rhyme (ABA) and a concluding quatrain rhyming ABAA. There is also a repeated line scheme: the first line returns at the end of stanza 2 and 4 and as the second-last line. Line three ends stanzas 3 and 5 and 6. An enormously impressive use of villanelle is Dylan Thomas' "Do Not Go Gentle." Thomas repeats the rhymes "night–day–light," the emotion accumulating in their very repetition, until they together flood the concluding quatrain in an unforgettable elegiac cry:

Do not go gentle into that good night,
Old age should burn and rave at close of day;
Rage, rage against the dying of the light.

Though wise men at their end know dark is right,
Because their words had forked no lightning they
Do not go gentle into that good night.

Good men, the last wave by, crying how bright
Their frail deeds might have danced in a green bay,
Rage, rage against the dying of the light.

Wild men who caught and sang the sun in flight,
And learn, too late, they grieved it on its way,
Do not go gentle into that good night.

Grave men, near death, who see with blinding sight
Blind eyes could blaze like meteors and be gay,
Rage, rage against the dying of the light.

And you, my father, there on the sad height,
Curse, bless, me now with your fierce tears, I pray.
Do not go gentle into that good night.
Rage, rage against the dying of the light.

The opening stanza announces the admonition, as the following stanzas announce four kinds of men who resist "the dying of the light." By rhyming "night," "light," "right," "bright," "flight," and "height," Thomas insures we hear the rhymed words as well as the tension between them—from brightness to the dark of death—so the insistence to "rage against" is also contained inside the rhyming. The words "day" and "they," while rhymed, are varied in emphasis by adept line breaks that shift the stress on each; the "-ay" rhyme takes on fresh weight with the final "pray." We hear the poem concluding with the address "And you, my father" and its four-line reiteration of rhyme words and lines.

Form in Elegy and Ode

Such fixed form poems as the above have both an external form and an internal energy, invented at some period in history to achieve specific ends. Some ancient forms, however, do not so much show an on-the-page visible form as a unique internal form. The elegy, for example, was developed to honor the deceased and to help the living to manage loss and find consolation in the face of death. Elegy introduces all the age-old questions: Why did she die? Why at a young age? Why did no one prevent his death? Our own sorrow, confusion, and anger all need to be resolved before we leave the dead in peace and go onward with life. The form of elegy, then, takes on the process of grief, often from near-despair, through a range of emotions, to a recognition that something else (depending on one's faith) may be in operation apart from private earthly sorrow. Finally comes acceptance. The outward shape is not uniform, but elegy possesses certain characteristics which repeat through the ages.

The ancient classical, pastoral elegy sought comfort in nature's returning cycles of vegetable death and regeneration. Natural cycles being apparent to us, the imagination utilizes them to reach toward the unknown and unseen, often toward the spiritual; thus certain flowers become symbols for life and death.

The earliest forms of elegy we call pastoral because they feature shepherds in rural settings surrounded by sheep. The Christian elegy claimed this imagery, Christ being the Good Shepherd, but, like classical elegy, it recognized that natural cycles, while crucial to our lives, are not sufficient to quell our grief. Vegetation stays in and of the earth: tulips bloom, die, and bloom again each spring. But humans die and do not return. Consequently, the elegy desires to reach beyond nature's mere repetition toward some kind of stable permanence, a form of afterlife. So, while elegy retains nature imagery as a figure of resurrection or rebirth, it often posits a spiritual world where eternal life (an end that gives meaning to death) is found, the objects of nature becoming emblems or symbols of afterlife.

Though without a set external structure, elegy does reflect the movement of the experience of grief. It is this experiential progression one hears in elegy, for example, in John Milton's "Lycidas," considered one of the most remarkable poems in the language. It begins like this:

> Yet once more, O ye laurels, and once more
> Ye myrtles brown, with ivy never sere,
> I come to pluck your berries harsh and crude,
> And with forc'd fingers rude,
> Shatter your leaves before the mellowing year.
> Bitter constraint, and sad occasion dear,
> Compels me to disturb your season due:
> For Lycidas is dead, dead ere his prime,
> Young Lycidas, and hath not left his peer.

As we saw in chapter two, the emotion lies in the descending sounds of "Yet once more," and continues setting the emotional tenor: "sere," "harsh and crude," "forced fingers rude." The speaker must sing for the dead friend, must shed a "melodious tear," must create, that is, a formal elegiac work. His gentle musing upon their boyhood lives together leads only to sharper pain of loss:

> But O the heavy change, now thou art gone,
> Now thou art gone and never must return!
>
> (lines 37–38)

The speaker calls upon the vegetative world's experience of death, but that only leads to further sorrow and anger that no water spirits came to help: "Where were ye, nymphs?" His mind then turns to other water gods, Lycidas having drowned in the Irish Sea, and to near-despair: perhaps I too will die soon, while too young to have done anything: Why bother trying to be a poet?

Consolation begins as he reconsiders water gods, for one at least is the god of the river Cam (where they attended university); another is St. Peter (who takes time to condemn bad clergy). The fact that water gods both descend and ascend (the "fountain Arethuse") suggests resurrection, as does the vegetable world which renews each year. With one last vision of the horror of Lycidas's drowned body (at "the bottom of the monstrous world"), the speaker accepts that death is not an end, for there is heavenly resurrection: Lycidas will reign as a star forever, to assist those "that wander in that perilous flood." His tear being shed, the song being sung, the speaker can return, consoled, to his daily, earthly world: "Tomorrow to fresh woods, and pastures new."

Here is the entire poem.

> *Lycidas*
>
> *In this Monody the Author bewails a learned Friend, unfortunately drowned in his Passage from Chester on the Irish Seas, 1637. And by occasion, foretells the ruin of our corrupted Clergy then in their height.*
>
> YET once more, O ye laurels, and once more,
> Ye myrtles brown, with ivy never sere,
> I come to pluck your berries harsh and crude,
> And with forced fingers rude,
> Shatter your leaves before the mellowing year.   5

Bitter constraint and sad occasion dear,
Compels me to disturb your season due:
For Lycidas is dead, dead ere his prime,
Young Lycidas, and hath not left his peer.
Who would not sing for Lycidas? he knew   10
Himself to sing, and build the lofty rhyme.
He must not float upon his watery bier
Unwept, and welter to the parching wind,
Without the meed of some melodious tear.
    Begin, then, Sisters of the sacred well,   15
That from beneath the seat of Jove doth spring,
Begin, and somewhat loudly sweep the string.
Hence with denial vain, and coy excuse,
So may some gentle Muse
With lucky words favour my destined urn,   20
And as he passes turn,
And bid fair peace be to my sable shroud.
For we were nursed upon the self-same hill,
Fed the same flock, by fountain, shade, and rill.
    Together both, ere the high lawns appeared   25
Under the opening eyelids of the morn,
We drove afield, and both together heard
What time the gray-fly winds her sultry horn,
Battening our flocks with the fresh dews of night,
Oft till the star that rose, at evening, bright   30
Toward heaven's descent had sloped his westering wheel.
Meanwhile the rural ditties were not mute,
Tempered to the oaten flute;
Rough satyrs danced, and fauns with cloven heel
From the glad sound would not be absent long,   35
And old Damœtas loved to hear our song.
    But O the heavy change, now thou art gone,
Now thou art gone and never must return!
Thee, shepherd, thee the woods, and desert caves,
With wild thyme and the gadding vine o'ergrown,   40
And all their echoes mourn.
The willows, and the hazel copses green,

Shall now no more be seen,
Fanning their joyous leaves to thy soft lays.
As killing as the canker to the rose,   45
Or taint-worm to the weanling herds that graze,
Or frost to flowers, that their gay wardrobe wear,
When first the white-thorn blows;
Such, Lycidas, thy loss to shepherd's ear.
     Where were ye, nymphs, when the remorseless deep   50
Closed o'er the head of your loved Lycidas?
For neither were ye playing on the steep,
Where your old bards, the famous druids, lie,
Nor on the shaggy top of Mona high,
Nor yet where Deva spreads her wizard stream.   55
Ay me! I fondly dream
Had ye been there—for what could that have done?
What could the Muse herself that Orpheus bore,
The Muse herself, for her enchanting son
Whom universal nature did lament,   60
When by the rout that made the hideous roar,
His gory visage down the stream was sent,
Down the swift Hebrus to the Lesbian shore?
     Alas! what boots it with uncessant care
To tend the homely, slighted Shepherd's trade,   65
And strictly meditate the thankless Muse?
Were it not better done, as others use,
To sport with Amaryllis in the shade,
Or with the tangles of Neæra's hair?
Fame is the spur that the clear spirit doth raise   70
(That last infirmity of noble mind)
To scorn delights and live laborious days;
But the fair guerdon when we hope to find,
And think to burst out into sudden blaze,
Comes the blind Fury with the abhorrèd shears,   75
And slits the thin-spun life. "But not the praise,"
Phœbus replied, and touched my trembling ears;
"Fame is no plant that grows on mortal soil,
Nor in the glistering foil

Set off to the world, nor in broad rumour lies,   80
But lives and spreads aloft by those pure eyes
And perfect witness of all-judging Jove;
As he pronounces lastly on each deed,
Of so much fame in heaven expect thy meed."
    O fountain Arethuse, and thou honoured flood,   85
Smooth-sliding Mincius, crowned with vocal reeds,
That strain I heard was of a higher mood.
But now my oat proceeds,
And listens to the Herald of the Sea,
That came in Neptune's plea.   90
He asked the waves, and asked the felon winds,
What hard mishap hath doomed this gentle swain?
And questioned every gust of rugged wings
That blows from off each beaked promontory.
They knew not of his story,   95
And sage Hippotades their answer brings,
That not a blast was from his dungeon strayed,
The air was calm, and on the level brine
Sleek Panope with all her sisters played.
It was that fatal and perfidious bark,   100
Built in the eclipse, and rigged with curses dark,
That sunk so low that sacred head of thine.
    Next Camus, reverend Sire, went footing slow,
His mantle hairy, and his bonnet sedge,
Inwrought with figures dim, and on the edge   105
Like to that sanguine flower inscribed with woe.
"Ah! who hath reft," quoth he, "my dearest pledge?"
Last came, and last did go,
The pilot of the Galilean lake;
Two massy keys he bore of metals twain   110
(The golden opes, the iron shuts amain).
He shook his mitred locks, and stern bespake:
"How well could I have spared for thee, young swain,
Enow of such as, for their bellies' sake,
Creep, and intrude, and climb into the fold?   115
Of other care they little reckoning make

Than how to scramble at the shearers' feast,
And shove away the worthy bidden guest.
Blind mouths! that scarce themselves know how to hold
A sheep-hook, or have learnt aught else the least   120
That to the faithful herdman's art belongs!
What recks it them? What need they? They are sped;
And, when they list, their lean and flashy songs
Grate on their scrannel pipes of wretched straw;
The hungry sheep look up, and are not fed,   125
But, swoln with wind and the rank mist they draw,
Rot inwardly, and foul contagion spread;
Besides what the grim Wolf with privy paw
Daily devours apace, and nothing said.
But that two-handed engine at the door   130
Stands ready to smite once, and smite no more."
    Return, Alpheus; the dread voice is past
That shrunk thy streams; return, Sicilian muse,
And call the vales, and bid them hither cast
Their bells and flowerets of a thousand hues.   135
Ye valleys low, where the mild whispers use
Of shades, and wanton winds, and gushing brooks,
On whose fresh lap the swart star sparely looks,
Throw hither all your quaint enamelled eyes,
That on the green turf suck the honeyed showers,   140
And purple all the ground with vernal flowers.
Bring the rathe primrose that forsaken dies,
The tufted crow-toe, and pale jessamine,
The white pink, and the pansy freaked with jet,
The glowing violet,   145
The musk-rose, and the well-attired woodbine,
With cowslips wan that hang the pensive head,
And every flower that sad embroidery wears;
Bid amaranthus all his beauty shed,
And daffodillies fill their cups with tears,   150
To strew the laureate hearse where Lycid lies.
For so, to interpose a little ease,
Let our frail thoughts dally with false surmise.

Ay me! whilst thee the shores and sounding seas
Wash far away, where'er thy bones are hurled;   155
Whether beyond the stormy Hebrides,
Where thou perhaps under the whelming tide
Visit'st the bottom of the monstrous world;
Or whether thou, to our moist vows denied,
Sleep'st by the fable of Bellerus old,   160
Where the great vision of the guarded mount
Looks toward Namancos and Bayona's hold.
Look homeward angel now, and melt with ruth:
And, O ye dolphins, waft the hapless youth.
    Weep no more, woeful shepherds, weep no more,   165
For Lycidas, your sorrow, is not dead,
Sunk though he be beneath the watery floor;
So sinks the day-star in the ocean bed,
And yet anon repairs his drooping head,
And tricks his beams, and with new-spangled ore   170
Flames in the forehead of the morning sky:
So Lycidas sunk low, but mounted high,
Through the dear might of Him that walked the waves,
Where, other groves and other streams along,
With nectar pure his oozy locks he laves,   175
And hears the unexpressive nuptial song,
In the blest kingdoms meek of joy and love.
There entertain him all the Saints above,
In solemn troops, and sweet societies,
That sing, and singing in their glory move,   180
And wipe the tears for ever from his eyes.
Now, Lycidas, the shepherds weep no more;
Henceforth thou art the Genius of the shore,
In thy large recompense, and shalt be good
To all that wander in that perilous flood.   185
    Thus sang the uncouth swain to the oaks and rills,
While the still morn went out with sandals gray:
He touched the tender stops of various quills,
With eager thought warbling his Doric lay;

> And now the sun had stretched out all the hills,   190
> And now was dropt into the western bay;
> At last he rose, and twitched his mantle blue:
> Tomorrow to fresh woods, and pastures new.

While Walt Whitman's elegy on the death of President Lincoln does not follow all the traditional patterns of Milton's poem, "When Lilacs Last in the Dooryard Bloom'd" does incorporate nature images of flower, star, and bird:

> When lilacs last in the dooryard bloom'd,
> And the great star early dropp'd in the western sky in the night,
> I mourn'd and yet shall mourn with ever-returning spring.
> Ever-returning spring, trinity sure to me you bring
> Lilac blooming perennial and drooping star in the west
> And thought of him I love.

A sense of violence appears, "A sprig with its flower I break," and then we hear "Solitary the thrush" which "sang the carol of death, and a verse for him I love." After tracing the procession of the coffin across the country, the speaker's song (Milton's was a monody, a solo song) of elegy concludes: "I cease from my song for thee, . . . Lilac and star and bird twined with the chant of my soul."

At the heart of elegy there seems to reside our world of nature as one progresses through sorrow, anger, and distress to peace, reconciliation, and consolation.

Patrick Kavanagh's "In Memory of my Mother" does not descend into overt sorrow and anger. Rather, with obviously Christian references to attending Mass, it creates a strongly affirmative memory of his late mother.

> I do not think of you lying in the wet clay
> Of a Monaghan graveyard; I see
> You walking down a lane among the poplars
> On your way to the station, or happily
>
> Going to second Mass on a summer Sunday—
> You meet me and you say:
> 'Don't forget to see about the cattle—'
> Among your earthiest words the angels stray.

And I think of you walking along a headland
Of green oats in June,
So full of repose, so rich with life—
And I see us meeting at the end of a town

On a fair day by accident, after
The bargains are all made and we can walk
Together through the shops and stalls and markets
Free in the oriental streets of thought.

O you are not lying in the wet clay,
For it is a harvest evening now and we
Are piling up the ricks against the moonlight
And you smile up at us—eternally.

He sees her in an almost ideal (pastoral), live world of sunlight, farmland animals, grain, town fairs and markets. Beautifully incorporating life and afterlife—"Among your earthiest words the angels stray"—there is both a sense of loss and a refusal to accept death as final. Nature's harvest becomes a figure for life's completion and eternal rest, as well as acceptance—"you are not lying in the wet clay"—and transcendence to her eternal smile.

The Jewish mourner's prayer is called Kaddish, to be recited regularly for eleven months for a dead parent. David Ignatow's poem for his mother contains elements of the natural, the earth, which he figuratively expands into continuing sustenance and strength: his mother was rock and stone.

Kaddish

Mother of my birth, for how long were we together
in your love and my adoration of your self?
For the shadow of a moment, as I breathed your pain
and you breathed my suffering. As we knew
of shadows in lit rooms that would swallow the light.

Your face beneath the oxygen tent was alive
but your eyes closed, your breathing hoarse.
Your sleep was with death. I was alone
with you as when I was young
but now only alone, not with you,
to become alone forever, as I was learning
watching you become alone.

Earth now is your mother, as you were mine, my earth,
my sustenance and my strength,
and now without you I turn to your mother
and seek from her that I may meet you again
in rock and stone. Whisper to the stone,
I love you. Whisper to the rock, I found you.
Whisper to the earth, Mother, I have found her,
and I am safe and always have been.

In both poems, nature/earth, afterlife, and consolation seem to be the essentials of elegy.

While we consider elegy here in its own form, there are elegiac poems without the formal process of grief. There are many ways to mourn, and the term "elegiac verse" covers a wide range of topics.

Here is Ben Jonson's touching memorial of his son (1603):

On My First Son

Farewell, thou child of my right hand, and joy;
My sin was too much hope of thee, lov'd boy.
Seven years thou were lent to me, and I thee pay,
Exacted by thy fate, on the just day.
O, could I lose all father now! For why
Will man lament the state he should envy?
To have so soon 'scap'd world's and flesh's rage,
And, if no other misery, yet age?
Rest in soft peace, and, ask'd, say, "Here doth lie
Ben Jonson his best piece of poetry."
For whose sake, henceforth, all his vows be such,
As what he loves may never like too much.

The final form we will take up (another ancient one), the ode, retains the external form of its origin in the hands of Greek poet Pindar. Because the ode, which means song (mentioned in chapter one, "Stanza"), is structured like a dance, it is divided into three stanzas called strophes or turns, as in a choral dance on stage: the strophe (move) is followed by the antistrophe (return), and the epode (stand or end). The ode begins with an assertion of praise, reflects on or questions the person and event, then concludes with reiterated praise.

In "To Autumn," John Keats numbered his ode's three stanzas: the first (strophe) is an adulation of the season of harvest, the second (antistrophe or counter-turn) wonders if autumn is a touch overrated, the third (epode or stand) returns to praise its birdsongs:

I

Season of mists and mellow fruitfulness,
   Close bosom-friend of the maturing sun;
Conspiring with him how to load and bless
   With fruit the vines that round the thatch-eaves run;
To bend with apples the mossed cottage-trees,
   And fill all fruit with ripeness to the core;
     To swell the gourd, and plump the hazel shells
   With a sweet kernel; to set budding more,
And still more, later flowers for the bees,
Until they think warm days will never cease,
   For summer has o'er-brimmed their clammy cell.

II

Who hath not seen thee oft amid thy store?
   Sometimes whoever seeks abroad may find
Thee sitting careless on a granary floor,
   Thy hair soft-lifted by the winnowing wind;
Or on a half-reaped furrow sound asleep,
   Drowsed with the fume of poppies, while thy hook
     Spares the next swath and all its twined flowers;
And sometimes like a gleaner thou dost keep
   Steady thy laden head across a brook;
   Or by a cider-press, with patient look,
     Thou watchest the last oozings hours by hours.

III

Where are the songs of spring? Ay, where are they?
   Think not of them, thou hast thy music too,—
While barred clouds bloom the soft-dying day,
   And touch the stubble-plains with rosy hue;
Then in a wailful choir the small gnats mourn
   Among the river sallows, borne aloft

> Or sinking as the light wind lives or dies;
> And full-grown lambs loud bleat from hilly bourn;
> Hedge-crickets sing; and now with treble soft
> The redbreast whistles from a garden-croft;
> And gathering swallows twitter in the skies.

The initial stanza's praise of autumn's sensuous fullness, its almost delicious excess, hesitates at the antistrophe to entertain a different perspective: is it merely "sitting careless," "sound asleep," "drowsed with the fume of poppies," as if sated in its bounty? The stand then confirms our pleasure in autumn: it has its music, in fact, an abundance of animal choirs! Keats's images in this tripartite model are so lavish in sight and sound that we readily hear in each of the three stages his celebration of autumn, and in the stand, we hear every creature's literal exuberance of song.

There is also a tradition of ode which does not follow the form deriving from Pindar. A more informal ode was composed by the Roman poet Horace. Many odes in English follow the Horatian model, open-ended as to form. The poem to Stephen Dowling Botts (from *Huckleberry Finn,*) is titled ode (chapter seven, "Rhyme"). The English seventeenth and eighteenth centuries were filled with odes, such as John Dryden's "Alexander's Feast, or The Power of Music. An Ode in Honour of St. Cecilia's Day," or Thomas Gray's comic "Ode on the Death of a favorite Cat, Drowned in a Tub of Goldfishes." William Collins wrote a series of both Pindaric ("Ode on the Poetical Character" in three numbered parts) and Horatian odes. His brief "Ode Written in the Beginning of the Year 1746" is also elegiac in tone:

> How sleep the brave who sink to rest,
> By all their country's wishes blest!
> When Spring, with dewy fingers cold,
> Returns to deck their hallowed mould,
> She there shall dress a sweeter sod
> Than Fancy's feet have ever trod.
>
> By fairy hands their knell is rung;
> By forms unseen their dirge is sung;
> There Honour comes, a pilgrim grey,
> To bless the turf that wraps their clay;

And Freedom shall awhile repair
To dwell a weeping hermit there!

In such poems, form is determined by the poem itself, for instance the procession of mourners in this last ode, Spring, Fancy, Honour, and Freedom, come to lay a wreath on the grave of brave soldiers.

Chapter Nine

Allegory, Symbol, and Allusion

Both *allegory* and *symbol* have their starting point with a specific object which is then related to something else, often an abstraction, as if the object reminds us of a feeling, or a smell, for instance. In allegory, the interest falls less on the object itself and more on the application. In symbol, interest falls equally on the object and its reference to an abstraction. An abstraction is a concept, an ideology, a manner of acting or code of behavior, such as selfishness, fascism, childrearing—not a specific object like a stone or bird. Similar as allegory and symbol may seem in their relation to objects, it is important to distinguish them in our discussions of poetry, or of any literature, so that they will have distinct and applicable meanings. We take up allusion afterwards.

In the previous chapter, on Form, we emphasized how one can hear form. In this present treatment of allegory and symbol, we do not feel it is necessary to call attention so explicitly to ways that one hears these forms, both being processes which we can detect and follow by ear as well as by mind.

Allegory and the Abstract

We begin with a poem by Russell Edson, "In All the Days of My Childhood," to observe what figurative methods Edson uses to address certain issues of childhood:

My father by some strange conjunction had mice for sons.

. . . And so it was in all the days of my childhood. . . . The winds blew, and then abated, the rains fell, and then climbed slowly back to heaven as vapor.

Day became night as night became day in rhythmic lengthenings and shortenings.

Time of the blossoming, and time of decline.

The sense of permanence broken by sudden change.

The time of change giving way again to a sense of permanence.

In the summer my brothers' tails dragged in the grass. What is more natural than their tails in the grass?

Upon their haunches, front paws feebly paddling air, whiskers twitching, they looked toward father with mindless faith.

In the winter father would pick them up by their tails and put them in cages.

The ping of snow on the windows; bad weather misunderstood. . . . Perhaps all things misunderstood?

It was that understanding came to no question.

Without a sense of the arbitrary no process of logic was instigated by my brothers. Was this wrong?

Again in the spring we moved out of doors, and again dragged our tails in the grass, looking toward father with mindless faith.

. . . And so it was in all the days of my childhood.

A man's sons are likened to mice. This likening is not a simile (which compares two things by *like* or *as*: this dog sleeps like a log); the figure links the behavior of sons toward their father with a single aspect of mouse behavior that is understood by all of us. Unlike simile, the likening is expanded and developed to reveal the full implications of the sons' behavior.

After the initial identification of sons with mice, nothing more is said about mousiness until their "tails dragged in the grass." Yes, the boys have paws and whiskers, but what matters about the conjunction of sons and mice is the stereotypical image of mice as feeble: the sons were like mice as creatures that timidly follow and blankly obey. Edson's speaker wants to investigate his brothers' dull obedience, so allegory sets up the mouse-son pairing in order to show how the father teaches a compliance that is destructive of their humanity. Even the son-speaker is infected: he seems to dodder along with his brothers: "in the spring we moved out of doors, and again dragged our tails in the grass, looking toward father with mindless faith." While allegory begins with an object, it focuses on the abstraction. As allegory, we learn very little about the nature of mice but a good deal about the timidity of the boys.

There is sufficient detail in this little story that we are able to hear and follow the progress of the sons; the questions also advance the story: What will they answer? Where will this lead? Surely the speaker will break away!

Allegory may use as referent a known historical, political, or literary (e.g., Biblical) story. In his novel *Animal Farm* (1954), George Orwell examined a society of pigs as a window into the nature of the historical phenomenon of Communism, specifically Soviet. We do not read *Animal Farm* to learn about pigs (although these pigs may be more devious and vicious than we had imagined). Rather, the behavior of pigs illuminates his real concern: the profoundly damaging effects of Communism. Even if we knew little about Communism, Orwell's allegory instructs us through the progression of the pigs' intolerant behavior. If Orwell wanted, he could have written an essay on the evils of Communism, but his choice of allegory keeps the pig motif before us, structures his narrative, enhances interest, and supplies a critical attitude that requires no explanation about Communism's social and economic structure.

John Bunyan's *Pilgrim's Progress* (1678–84) tells the story of the man Christian whose travels and travails parallel in allegory the life of any Christian. Bunyan's interest was the life of a Christian person, not on specifics of the man Christian's domestic life. Again, through the depth of his analysis, Bunyan reveals a great deal of the nature of Christian life, in case we do not know the referent, whether historical or other.

It often takes some time for an allegory to explain the complexities of the abstraction—cause and effects of the sons' behavior, the development of Communism, the journey of a Christian life. Allegory is thus often a detailed narrative about the abstraction, whereas a symbol ordinarily requires little exposition.

Symbolic Thinking

Although we can speak of stories as symbols, and even words and numbers as symbols, *symbol* is traditionally defined as *an object that stands for something other than itself.* (An object cannot symbolize itself: a collie does not symbolize a dog.) As distinct from allegory (Edson's mouse is not developed), in symbolism our attention is focused equally on the object and on its application. Both are developed.

In our earlier discussion, several objects in Bly's "My Father's Wedding, 1924" were left unaddressed: the breast, the drops, and poison.

> In her left
> breast she carried the three drops
> that wound and kill.

The breast is a literal site of life and nourishment, and the left side links it with the heart (not mentioned) which also gives life. (The heart does *not* symbolize the blood-pumping muscle: it *is* that.) So the heart *stands for* the organ of life and the breast *stands for* the organ of nourishment (particularly for an infant).

The father's fixation on breast draws it away from heart, which he should see as symbolic of her physical and spiritual being. For him it is the breast that has "the three drops / that wound and kill," the symbolic power to destroy, to not nourish. The number three itself frequently signifies/symbolizes the spiritual or the good (e.g., a perfect number, Trinity, the triangle's strength). But like anything else, the symbolic power of three can be subverted, as it is, for example, with the three weird sisters in *Macbeth*. The father here does not regard the value of breast or heart: he de-symbolizes them. Until he corrects his error and sees both heart and breast as they actually are and in their distinct, true symbolic meanings, he will remain subject to infection—not from a vial of bodily poison but through a psychological one—which will kill his spirit.

In "Tree" (from *Remains of Elmet*, 1979) Ted Hughes explores symbolic thinking with an eye to the perils of not seeing objects and thus being incapable of symbolic thought.

> A priest from a different land
> Fulminated
> Against heather, black stones, blown water.

Excommunicated the clouds
Damned the wind
Cast the bog pools into outer darkness
Smote the horizons
With the jawbone of emptiness

Till he ran out of breath—

In that teetering moment
Of lungs empty
When only his eye-water protected him
He saw
Heaven and earth moving.

And words left him.
Mind left him. God left him.

Bowed—
The lightning conductor
Of a maiming glimpse—the new prophet—

Under unending interrogation by wind
Tortured by huge scaldings of light
Tried to confess all but could not
Bleed a word

Stripped to his root-letter, cruciform
Contorted
Tried to tell all

Through crooking of elbows
Twitching of finger-ends.

Finally
Resigned
To be dumb.

Lets what happens to him simply happen.

Hughes does not isolate a single object but enumerates "heather, black stones, blown water," later "bog pools," in their particular landscape. These objects the priest refuses to recognize as knowable or containing symbolic potential: they are essentially dead to him.

Railing (playing God, Biblically) against objects in order to drive them away from him and away from meaning (as if he is indeed seeking "emptiness"), the priest can do nothing but exhaust himself. In spite of his furor—bereft even of words, let alone of mind and God—Heaven and earth do continue to move, and nature decides to give him a terrific reminder of the perils of denying its power:

> Under unending interrogation by wind
> Tortured by huge scaldings of light.

Nature thus does act. It does have meaning: the wind *questions*, the light *burns*. Through his rejection of objects and their meaning, and thus of the meaning and value of symbol, the priest stands (having suffered an almost comically thorough thrashing) unable to move anything but his fingertips. Being wordless, he has abandoned human means to address this world, and has certainly abandoned any chance to ascend to mind and to God (as priest, he ought to know the importance of the Word). Symbolic thinking, Hughes implies, is a natural process of mind, of making sense of things of the world: in order to exist and survive we humans need to see value and meaning in things. The village of Elmet is nothing but the remains of a mill-town, ruined, Hughes suggests, because the materials of nature were denied their meaning and value, and thus were exploited to ruin.

Religious symbols are objects that stand for the central aspects of a belief: a cross, a scimitar, a five-pointed star. Such symbolic objects are usually recognizable, but may require a certain amount of explanation. For instance, in a stained glass window, a pelican pecking blood from its breast to feed its young is a symbol of Jesus sacrificing his blood to sustain his people. Numbers can have symbolic meanings: three often stands for the spiritual, whereas four is the earthly—four seasons, four directions, the four elements of earth, fire, air, and water. In Keats's "La Belle Dame sans Merci" specific numbers are mentioned: the knight being much attached to earth gives her "kisses *four*," whereas she, a fairy, hands him *three* gifts: roots, honey, and manna. Multiples are also symbolic: 3 x 3 is 9; 3 x 4 is 12. Ten is perfection, as is one. The symbolism of 666 is common knowledge: Satanic.

Allusion

In the poems we have been reading, the poem itself usually establishes its intended metaphoric connections. Ted Hughes' terms are explicit: priest, heather, stones, storms. But in some cases the figurative connection is not formally made and associated meanings may escape us. For example, in Denise Levertov's "Where is the Angel" (quoted in full in chapter one) we read:

> Where is the angel for me to wrestle?
> No driving snow in the glass bubble,
> but mild September.

We know what an angel is and what wrestling is, but the poem does not explain why the speaker is wrestling an angel. The angel-wrestle image is an *allusion, a* reference to an unnamed story, event, person. The book of Genesis (chapter 32) tells of Jacob wrestling an angel and being wounded in the thigh. To this Levertov alludes:

> to wrestle with me and wound
> not my thigh but my throat,
> so curses and blessings flow storming out. . . .

A clue to the existence of allusion is precisely the expansion of an image without explanation, as she expands to wounding "not my thigh but my throat."

Allusion enriches a reference or image by implying or suggesting another context of meaning. Western poetry is filled with allusions to the Bible and texts like those of Homer, Dante, Shakespeare, Milton, Yeats, T. S. Eliot. For example, if we encounter a conscious reference—not a vague passing mention—to an indecisive person, the allusion may be to Hamlet. A story of a fall from spiritual or religious grace could refer to Adam's and Eve's fall in the *Bible* or in *Paradise Lost*. A descent by stages into a place of despair may allude to Dante's *Inferno*. Levertov amplifies the significance of her battle beyond everyday writer's block by alluding to Jacob's momentous struggle with an angel and the wound which is the mark of spiritual endeavor.

Seamus Heaney's "Limbo" unfolds a cluster of allusions, references he does not explain.

> Fishermen at Ballyshannon
> Netted an infant last night
> Along with the salmon.
> An illegitimate spawning,

A small one thrown back
To the waters. But I'm sure
As she stood in the shallows
Ducking him tenderly

Till the frozen knobs of her wrists
Were dead as the gravel,
He was a minnow with hooks
Tearing her open.

She waded in under
The sign of her cross.
He was hauled in with the fish.
Now limbo will be

A cold glitter of souls
Through some far briny zone.
Even Christ's palms, unhealed,
Smart and cannot fish there.

Theologically, Limbo is the place where unbaptized infants are sent for the afterlife, since they have neither merited punishment for sin (Purgatory or Hell) nor salvation in Heaven, and the mark of Original Sin has not been washed away in baptism. In popular usage, limbo designates a place of uncertainty. Her drowned child will land in Limbo. She remains in a limbo of confusion. Hidden in the poem is the allusion that she is an Irish Catholic who adheres to this doctrine of Limbo and her dead child's fate. She also holds her "illegitimate" child (the product of forbidden sex outside of marriage) to be a sign of devastating shame (sin) and thus feels that killing her child is the better option. A further allusion lies in "The sign of her cross"—for while she would make the Christian sign of the cross with her hand, she also bears a cross of shame. Near the end, Christian allusions include Christ himself: if Christ died for us by crucifixion (nailed palms), then why is she not saved? Or her child? Why is he outcast in Limbo? Christ cannot raise her up by his hands. Christ is by allusion a fisher of souls: he cannot "fish there" in her damned soul, so his act of salvation is for naught: "A cold glitter of souls."

Allusion here not only creates the frame for her theological thinking but provides the speaker the means for questioning this harshly dismissive treatment of her and her child (whom she loves "tenderly"). The fish image (a Christian sign) persists; the fishhooks are also the child's claim on her, thus "tearing." But salmon, typically caught in these Irish waters, carries its own allusive, mythic weight: in Celtic mythology, the salmon means wisdom for its ability to trace its way home to spawn.

A single fact which may seem self-evident or incidental gathers depths of meaning when placed allusively in historical contexts. Mari Evans writes of herself as a black woman, and through allusion's great verbal economy she can expand this single fact into a complete history of herself.

I Am a Black Woman

I am a black woman
the music of my song
some sweet arpeggio of tears
is written in a minor key
and I
can be heard humming in the night
Can be heard
    humming
in the night

I saw my mate leap screaming to the sea
and I / with these hands / cupped the lifebreath
from my issue in the canebrake
I lost Nat's swinging body in a rain of tears
and heard my son scream all the way from Anzio
for Peace he never knew. . . . I
learned Da Nang and Pork Chop Hill
in anguish
Now my nostrils know the gas
and these trigger tire / d fingers
seek the softness in my warrior's beard

I am a black woman
tall as a cypress
strong
beyond all definition still

defying place
and time
and circumstance
   assailed
     impervious
         indestructible
Look
on me and be
renewed

Beginning with "I saw" she flashes vignettes of black history, Africans leaping off slave ships, the "canebrake" of Southern slave workplaces. "Nat's swinging body" recalls the rebellious slave Nat Turner who was hanged; Anzio is a WWII beachhead for the invasion of Italy where black troops were conspicuous for bravery; Pork Chop Hill was a Korean War battle; Da Nang remembers black troops in Vietnam. But since her history is a woman's and has been rarely recorded, to celebrate her own is to celebrate her mate's history, for she participates in both. Her final stanza images herself as tall and permanent—"defying" rather than complicit, "impervious" rather than a weak and fragile thing of white stereotypes. The line "tall as a cypress" may allude to Angelina Weld Grimké's "The Black Finger" (1925):

I have just seen a beautiful thing
   Slim and still,
Against a gold, gold sky,
   A straight cypress,
   Sensitive
   Exquisite.

A black finger
Pointing upwards.
Why, beautiful, still finger are you black?
And why are you pointing upwards?

Grimké (1880–1958) also celebrated black women, and Evans, a participant in the Black Arts Movement of the 1970s, lays claim to woman's place in history by allusions that encompass black history.

Changing or Blending Figures

It is not always easy to say, "This is a symbol." "That is allegory." Poets are not bound to respect nice differences for our convenience. If we look, for example, into William Blake's "A Poison Tree" what we think is an allusion to the Edenic tree whose fruit tempted Adam and Eve may be only half or a third of the story.

> I was angry with my friend:
> I told my wrath, my wrath did end.
> I was angry with my foe:
> I told it not, my wrath did grow.
>
> And I water'd it in fears,
> Night & morning with my tears:
> And I sunned it with smiles
> And with soft deceitful wiles.
>
> And it grew both day and night.
> Till it bore an apple bright.
> And my foe beheld it shine,
> And he knew that it was mine,
>
> And into my garden stole
> When the night had veil'd the pole;
> In the morning glad I see
> My foe outstretch'd beneath the tree.

The poem images "my wrath" as a tree which the speaker waters and feeds, but the tree itself becomes less important (as in allegory) than cultivation of "my wrath." The bright, shining apple that emerges becomes a symbol of the speaker's powerfully internalized wrath (abstraction becomes physical object). But by stanza three, attention draws away from the apple toward the nature and purpose of the incarnated anger, almost as if the symbolic function of the apple slides back toward allegory. But allusion also keeps surfacing: is the tempting apple like the one in the Garden of Eden? If this is allusion to the tree of *Genesis*, we may think it strange, perhaps shocking, that the Creator would set a sly trick like this one to "get" the Edenic couple. The allusion would then ironically invert the standard

Genesis story of Adam and Eve falling through their own fault. Does this allusion depict God as "glad" to see his creatures "outstretched beneath the tree"? Or is the whole poem an allegory about the power of anger? Or is it about the demonic power of bringing abstract anger into actuality, Anger become Fruit, in parody of the creative power of the Word (Son of God) become Flesh (Jesus) in Christian theology? That the figures of this poem are not easily separated and individualized should not matter as long as they together create a distinctly imagined and felt whole.

Chapter Ten

Memory

n the introduction we said that memorizing a poem is an indispensable step to drawing in and holding its complete intellectual and emotional meaning. Through the work of memory, we come to terms with and solve almost all elements about a poem's prosody (line, sound, rhythm, meter, rhyme, and the like), its emotion and its meaning. We cannot dodge the problems of a poem as we learn to speak its words and lines and sentences with meaning, natural expression, and clarity. Most importantly, memorizing a poem draws it into our minds and into our bodies. Mind and body are together engaged: *learning by heart.* Learning how a poem works leads us to know what it is about. Simultaneously, learning what it is about leads us to know how it works.

A classroom episode might suggest the power of memorizing, in this case the personally physical ramifications of taking in a poem's emotion and rhythm. The experiences presented here ought not be viewed as unique to college students or to classroom work. What we describe here is representative of how memory work can be effective for anyone, and can have, as we say, physical and emotional impact. Fran Quinn was teaching war poetry, and one requirement of the course was that students memorize several poems. Though memory work was standard in his courses, the students rebelled loudly and uncharacteristically. They would memorize poems, yes, but not war poems. Why? They claimed they feared, simply, the emotional strain upon themselves of memorizing poems about the experience of war. One student wept as he (at last) recited. Allowing the rhythmic power of a poem into one's body and mind can be a unique, a changing, a perhaps fearful experience.[1]

Steps in Memorizing

There are no set rules on how to memorize, no golden method that works for each of us. There are, however, a few steps to assist the process of memory work which we have discovered to be effective. A handy dictionary will give the meaning of all the words and their pronunciation. Then as we read aloud we follow lines and the structure of the sentences to be sure how clauses and phrases become part of the whole sentence; in earlier English verse with complex sentence structures this may require close attention.

The first step in actual memorizing is to read the poem aloud a number of times until we grasp how the lines and stanzas move through the whole. This is important for beginners in memory work. During this reading, we correct such mistakes as wrong sentence structure and word emphasis, confused tempo, misplaced pitch, garbled sound effects, mistakes by no means unusual (mistakes are invariably instructive). From everything we have learned chapter by chapter about the elements of prosody, we know we rely on the poem itself to tell us what it means and how to say it. We listen to the way line moves, for example, or how sound directs us to hear meaning, and so on. However, we may also need an audience, someone to say: "No, you are confusing the rhythm with metrical beat." "You do not quite have the voice of the speaker." "Try to sound like a person talking, closer to natural speech."

Reading aloud the entire poem rather than part by separate part helps us to hear the poem as a unit and to forestall interrupting the rhythm and memory.[2]

As we train our ear and develop our abilities to speak and hear poems, we listen to our own voice for self-correction. But the speaker of the poem also has a voice. We try to approximate—not mimic—in our own voice the voice of the speaker. That may be challenging, especially if that voice is unlike our own, from a different part of the United States, or from Canada, or Slovenia. In such cases, we may very likely need an audience to listen for where we stray and tell us what and how to correct.

Achievement of Memory Work

In the process of memory work, some of us are going to be more responsive to sound, some to tempo, others to line breaks. Some may have to slow down hurried speech habits, others may have to enunciate words more clearly, and we all may have to listen better. For when we memorize poems, we have the surprising opportunity of discovering many more things in the poem than we ever thought possible. Memorizing a poem does not mean we are finished with it for good. Instead, the memorized poem continues to stay alive and ripe for further exploration, for we allow it to release more and more and we continue learning. As Czeslaw Milosz put it near the end of his *"Ars Poetica?"*

> The purpose of poetry is to remind us
> how difficult it is to remain just one person,
> for our house is open, there are no keys in the door,
> and invisible guests come in and out at will.

As we speak the poem, the emotional effects of its sounds and rhythms come through our memory and into our body—the very sounding of words rises in our voice with vocal resonance. Poet and classicist Anne Carson examines the juncture between oral and written cultures:

> . . . most of the data important to survival and understanding are channelled into the individual through the open conduits of his senses, particularly his sense of sound, in a continuous interaction linking him with the world outside him. . . . To close his senses off from the outside world would be counter-productive to life and to thought.
>
> . . . Reading and writing require focusing the mental attention upon a text by means of the visual sense. As an individual reads and writes he gradually learns to close or inhibit the input of his senses, to inhibit or control the responses of the body, so as to train energy and thought upon the written words.[3]

We will take rhythm as one illustration of the ways physicality emerges in oral recitation of poems. Rhythm is expressed in our voices. But it is also made manifest in our stance, our gestures, our physical movement. The body in fact often *knows* before the mind discovers. That priority became evident when a group of students was discussing Lawrence's "Snake." The question we raised was, what is being suggested in these lines?

> He reached down from a fissure in the earth-wall in the gloom
> And trailed his yellow-brown slackness soft-bellied down,
>   over the edge of the stone trough
> And rested his throat upon the stone bottom,
> And where the water had dripped from the tap, into a small clearness,
> He sipped with his straight mouth,
> Softly drank through his straight gums, into his slack long body,
> Silently.

A serpentine movement seemed apparent, but how do we talk about that, how do we isolate where and how it is taking place? The students felt constricted when explaining verbally, so quite naturally they had recourse to hands and bodies, swaying back and forth. Their bodies knew something was happening and gave insight. (In chapter three we explored how rise and fall of pitch in the poem guides the body's movement.)

Memorizing a poem takes us directly into the *experience* of how a poem moves, how part is linked to part, how sound and rhythm are incorporated in it. The poem comes alive inside our bodies, known and experienced, and its physicality transfers directly to our bodies: we move and gesture as we speak.

Take for example Robert Creeley's "The Flower":

> I think I grow tensions
> like flowers
> in a wood where
> nobody goes.
>
> Each wound is perfect,
> encloses itself in a tiny
> imperceptible blossom,
> making pain.
>
> Pain is a flower like that one,
> like this one,
> like that one,
> like this one.

In memorizing this poem we are conscious of pauses and of a need for gestures, as in the last lines: "like this one, / like that one / like this one."

Another poem we read (chapter one), Yeats's "Adam's Curse," shows the way vocal silences allow critical transitions between stanzas:

Adam's Curse

We sat together at one summer's end,
That beautiful mild woman, your close friend,
And you and I, and talked of poetry.
I said: "A line will take us hours maybe;
Yet if it does not seem a moment's thought,
Our stitching and unstitching has been naught.
Better go down upon your marrow-bones
And scrub a kitchen pavement, or break stones
Like an old pauper, in all kinds of weather;
For to articulate sweet sounds together
Is to work harder than all these, and yet
Be thought an idler by the noisy set
Of bankers, schoolmasters, and clergymen
The martyrs call the world."

                     And thereupon
That beautiful mild woman for whose sake
There's many a one shall find out all heartache
On finding that her voice is sweet and low
Replied: "To be born woman is to know—
Although they do not talk of it at school—
That we must labour to be beautiful."

I said: "It's certain there is no fine thing
Since Adam's fall but needs much labouring.
There have been lovers who thought love should be
So much compounded of high courtesy
That they would sigh and quote with learned looks
Precedents out of beautiful old books;
Yet now it seems an idle trade enough."

We sat grown quiet at the name of love;
We saw the last embers of daylight die,

And in the trembling blue-green of the sky
A moon, worn as if it had been a shell
Washed by time's waters as they rose and fell
About the stars and broke in days and years.

I had a thought for no one's but your ears:
That you were beautiful, and that I strove
To love you in the old high way of love;
That it had all seemed happy, and yet we'd grown
As weary-hearted as that hollow moon.

After "The martyrs call the world" a period marks the end of the speaker's statement. Then a distinct stanza-break pause before "And thereupon" prepares for the mild woman's reply (more than two lines occur before she actually begins). At her close and stanza break, the speaker must consider for a moment before he responds: "I said: . . ." Following his speech, a major pause for reflection is marked, like a stage direction:

We sat grown quiet at the name of love;
We saw the last embers of daylight die.

The sentiments and tempo here are slow and thoughtful, as they are also in the final stanza. As we memorize and recite "Adam's Curse," the poem tells us precisely when, of what duration, and with what emotional feeling we are to pause so that the drama of the poem lives.

Memory and Insight

Memorizing leads us deeply inside a poem, guiding us to continual discovery of it. For example, William Blake's *Songs of Innocence and of Experience* are short poems, often simple in appearance on the page, and simple in their named contents: nurses and babies, mothers and children, woods and pastures, lambs and trees. Sure, there are a few darkish poems, about gritty London and sooty chimneys, a few lost boys . . . , but the melodies are often cheery. Here is the opening poem, "Introduction," of *Songs of Innocence*:

Piping down the valleys wild,
    Piping songs of merry glee,
On a cloud I saw a child,
    And he laughing said to me

Nicely upbeat. The trochaic meter (accent–unaccent) is consistent, but the probable pauses in line four may give us some concern. Is the line to be spoken, "And he laughing" or "And he, laughing, said . . . "? The pauses slow or break the trochaic meter, signaling a change to accentuate the child's response and prepare for what was said to him.

Here is the complete poem "The Lilly":

> The modest rose puts forth a thorn,
> The humble sheep, a threat'ning horn:
> While the lilly white, shall in love delight,
> Nor a thorn nor a threat stain her beauty bright.

This seems a simple poem about a flower. But in line three the iambics begin to fade with an anapest before each iamb: "while the LIL-ly WHITE, shall in LOVE de-LIGHT." Were we to read line four as all anapests, "stain" would be unaccented even though its strong sound and its role as verb suggest it is emphatic: "neither one *stains* her beauty."

In this poem the metrical tensions are reinforced by—or reinforce—contrasts within the lines: the rose is modest but has thorns; the sheep is humble but exhibits a horn, as if our notion of such creatures may become simplistic. As we endeavor to speak the poems in natural speech patterns, we perceive that the metrical irregularities are integral aspects of the poems and that they likely illustrate Blake's concept of contraries (or tensions) which he announces in the full title: *Songs of Innocence and of Experience*, "Showing the two contrary states of the human soul." That is, when so much about the poems *appears* simple and childlike, their metrical contrariness keeps us off balance and forces us to confront complexity as we speak the lines.

If we learn to speak aloud Blake's *Songs* and thus learn much of what those poems are about, what happens when we look at another of his works, a long poem (comprising 45 hand-engraved and illustrated plates) in fourteen-syllable lines, titled simply *Milton*? Will speaking the poem aloud be in any way different and revealing of its meaning? Reading aloud even the following few lines is a distinctly different experience from intoning "Piping down the valleys wild."[4]

> And Milton said, I go to eternal death! The nations still
> Follow after the detestable gods of Priam; in pomp

Of warlike selfhood, contradicting and blaspheming.
When will the Resurrection come, to deliver the sleeping body
From corruptibility: O when Lord Jesus wilt thou come?

(Plate 14, lines 14–18)

What is the effect of our voice moving across lines of fourteen syllables, what rhythms do we hear, how do such lines tell us of the meaning of the poem? Through such comparison of Blake's poems, we reflect that while the metrical difficulties in *Songs* reinforce "the two contrary states of the human soul," the fourteen-syllable line of *Milton* sounds different in many ways: in length of presented statement, in tempo, rhythmic movement, sound, and dramatic effect of line breaks. What seems apparent is that Blake's goal in *Milton* is not to explore contraries but to declaim a prophetic statement, to lift us upward to vision of the Lord. Since one cannot easily declaim and prophesy in short lilting lines, the verse of *Milton* is more declarative, more explanatory, in places more incantatory, thus we say prophetic. It has prosodic muscularity.

Experience and Reflection

Having worked with our poetry students for many years, we were quite certain what their success in learning by heart had been, but we thought it would be useful to have them record their experience. To our call, they responded thoughtfully.

For one student, memorization obliged him to pay attention to "the practicalities" of lines, for upon such specifics he built the "foundation upon which to approach the ideas and broader implications of the work." Another wrote: "the parts which I found difficult were parts where there were nuances in the rhythm and phrasing" that made me realize "the poem had a meaning that differed from its surface level." Passages of a poem that were difficult to memorize often contained problematic prosody: lines might not be easy to remember because a change was taking place in the meter or the tempo, not because one's memory was faulty. One student learned that the voice or speaker of a poem had to be sustained to deliver the experience of the whole; memorizing for her "necessitated attention to each word"; then the "rhythm and flow of the narrative, the maze of words . . . all of a sudden have this final slamming impact." Another reflected:

"a college student like myself is inclined to draw/accept the lines around the subject matter of their lives. . . . [M]emorization encouraged me to engage the poetry from various different physical and mental spaces." Still another felt that memorizing Blake's long poem *Milton* "places you within Blake's mythic world in a way that reading alone does not. . . . Memorizing helps you realize how human and real Blake's concerns are." It was not surprising that our students would respond to memory work with such insight and sureness of understanding, for the mental and physical act of memory draws a poem's experience into personal actuality. "Once you've built your 'memory bank' of poems," wrote another, "reading a poem 'cold' is a much more comfortable and enlightening experience."[5]

As with Fran's student reciting war poetry, recitation can be transformative. One evening after a poetry reading by Ruth Stone, a group of us were sitting around a living room, students (first-year college), teachers, poets, friends, interested visitors. Someone suggested each of us recite a poem. So it started, one after another, the students first, since Ruth, sitting on a chair in their midst, was so encouraging to them. One young woman sitting on the floor said she would do Dylan Thomas' "Do Not Go Gentle." At her opening phrase, we knew that something extraordinary was taking place. Reciting it flawlessly, she moved so completely inside the poem, it was as if another voice were speaking. As she ended, she sat unmoving. No breath was drawn in the room. It was the most remarkable example of sheer verbal experience I—no doubt we all—had ever witnessed. Later, she said she did not really know what had happened to her or why. It had nothing to do with a death in the family or any recalled experience. It was the poem itself pure and simple. She had understood and felt the rhythms so fully that the poem took over her body and emotions.

Notes

1. In our emphasis on memory work in the study of poetry, we find ourselves in agreement with the observations of a lecture by poet Lucio Mariani:

   Public education in Italy has, for a long time, done away with the practice of memorizing poems, something now branded as a form of regressive pedagogy and a despicable teaching method. As a result, works by greater and lesser poets are only approached through the lens of the critic, who routinely dissects and comments on poems by placing them in theoretical and comparative contexts. . . .

In this way, students do not access the complex emotional pathways that repeated readings and memorization can open up. Thus the Dionysian nerve hidden in each of us does not get to the surface, let alone be stimulated. And as a result, the student does not get to have the admittedly difficult but extraordinary experience of knowing a poem directly, on one's own, even if in the silent mnemonic repetitions that are part and parcel of any and all learning, at every stage of life. Instead, the student will be forced to study the soul and signposts of a poem on the basis of commentaries that . . . [overshadow the poem], while the commentaries themselves become independent objects of study.

Lucio Mariani, "Concerning the Diffusion and Re-creation of Poetry: In Praise of the Lesser Players," *Literary Imagination* 7.1 (2005), 101.

2. In his indispensable book, *Playing Shakespeare,* John Barton points out that during rehearsal, an actor should be "very conscious of the verse" (though self-consciousness may be inhibiting) but should not think of it "in performance," where one has internalized the poem's words, lines, and rhythms, so that the poem flows without the struggle of conscious "memory" at work. (London, New York: Methuen, 1984, 44.)

3. For other aspects to this mind/body unity, see Anne Carson, *Eros, The Bittersweet*, pp.36–37. For important discussions of memory, see James McConkey, *The Anatomy of Memory, An Anthology.*

The history of memory is itself worth mention. Before printed texts became available, memory was the repository of knowledge. Oral cultures without written texts know this. Oral modes of understanding differ from those of a text culture. Not only Homer created long epic poems to be recited by bards or griots; almost every culture has, or had, a memory tradition. Even now, people memorize entire Broadway shows, song upon song upon song of their favorites: Cole Porter, George Gershwin, Fats Waller, U-2. Pianists memorize hosts of sonatas and concertos; actors memorize roles in many plays. In a remarkable study of medieval culture, *The Book of Memory*, Mary J. Carruthers describes the working of memory in Thomas Aquinas (13th century): contemporaries attest that he composed mentally, then dictated the compendious *Summa Theologica* from memory, without having drafted it first by himself. Such persons were trained to link together a series of texts to a Biblical phrase, ready for quick recall. In fact, well trained minds could compose on several topics simultaneously. Since John Milton was blind when he "wrote" *Paradise Lost* and other last poems, he had to dictate the poems stored in his memory to his amanuensis.

4. Colin Huerter (with permission: Holy Cross class of 2001) put it this way: "Blake seems to work through the body more, contort our faces and our extremities as we recite" the poems. "Just think of how different it is to recite [Wordsworth's] 'I wandered' and the 'Tyger.'"

5. With permission of (in order): Daniel Riley, Lauren Schnare, Sara D'Alessandro, Riley again, Patrick Tigue, Holy Cross College class of 2004.

Acknowledgments

This book began as a collection of notes for our Introduction to Poetry classes at Holy Cross, as Fran and I, team-teaching, tried to put into words what we wanted the students to understand about our approach to poems. It was also our attempt to find language for our efforts. Fran knew what he wanted the class to achieve, but our language was limited: how does one describe how the sounds of words have meaning? I needed to assign the students essays to write, but how could I expect them to discuss what we struggled to put into words? They, of course, helped us find language, for they quickly proved they could "hear" poems; they could recite them to us with meaning. Through that dynamic of interchange we found our way. This means that our first thanks go to those (mostly first-year) students who were so quick and willing and responsive. Whatever we were doing worked; they understood.

Fran and I talked and discussed and argued over drafts until clarity began to emerge. And so, chapter by chapter, the book evolved. My wife, Barbara, encouraged me while emphasizing the need to be clear and uncomplicated for our projected audience. Reaching those goals was frustratingly remote, until our agent, my nephew, Paul D. McCarthy (McCarthy Creative Services), suggested that we should eliminate academic arguments (such as: "Harold Bloom says this, but I disagree . . .") and just say what we believe. Much cutting later, we achieved what we hope is a clearer, more direct book.

Ordinary thanks are obviously insufficient for Barbara, and also for Paul. Nor are mere thanks sufficient for the grant from the Holy Cross College Research and Publication Committee, and for the generous contribution from President Rev. Philip Boroughs, S. J., to cover costs of permissions. Finally, Sid Hall kindly read the manuscript, believed in it, and took it on for publication. Thanks to all.

—B. E. McCarthy

Credits

Index

Index of First Lines

About the Authors

B. EUGENE MCCARTHY has a degree in English and a Master's from the University of Detroit. He took his PhD at the University of Kansas in 1965. He taught a full range of undergraduate courses at Holy Cross College until his retirement in 2000. His focus was on Restoration and Eighteenth Century drama, and his first book was *William Wycherley: A Biography* (Ohio University Press, 1979), followed by *William Wycherley, A Reference Guide* (G. K. Hall, 1985).

His interest then moved toward poetry of the 18th Century and he began teaching first-year, introductory courses in poetry, teaming with Fran Quinn to develop an approach to poetry that also informed upper-level literature courses.

As a visiting scholar at Clare Hall at Cambridge University, he researched *Thomas Gray: The Progress of a Poet* (Fairleigh Dickinson University Press, 1997). Several other publications came out of his study of Gray. "Reading Blake: A Case for Memorization" appeared in *Interfaces: Image, Texte, Language* (2010).

While publishing in African American literature on Richard Wright and Toni Morrison, his most recent work was co-edited with Thomas L. Doughton, *From Bondage to Belonging: The Worcester Slave Narratives* (U. Mass Press, 2007), an edition of eight narratives by ex-slaves who lived in Worcester. He has been an editor of *The Worcester Review* and participates in the Milton Ensemble which offers dramatic performances of books of *Paradise Lost* each year.

In recent years he has taught poetry and literature in the Worcester Institute for Senior Education (WISE) program at Assumption College. Since retirement, he and his wife, Barbara (Humanities Department, WPI), enjoy hiking, foreign travel, visiting their five children and nine grandchildren. They continue their interest in reading, and often, with friends, attend music, film, and theater in the Worcester and Boston areas. His interest in watercoloring absorbs much pleasurable time and attention.

FRAN QUINN has a bachelor's degree from Assumption College and an ABD from U. Mass, Amherst. He taught literature in high schools and in colleges in New England for many years. His interest was always in finding innovative ways to teach poetry to students at various levels—ways to allow the students to discover and learn, and bring them inside poems, not keep them outside, without emotional engagement.

Most important to this teaching is that he is a poet himself; he published three volumes of poetry, *Milk of the Lioness* (1982), *The Goblet Crying for Wine* (Blue Sofa Press, 1995), and *A Horse of Blue Ink* (Blue Sofa Press, 2005), and has placed poems in various journals. In 2002, *The Worcester Review* produced a special issue for his 60th birthday with forty tributes by such poets as Robert Bly, Eavan Boland, Coleman Barks, Seamus Heaney, and Galway Kinnell. Robert Creeley says, "Fran has been and is the best news possible"; says Donald Hall, "No one has worked so hard for poetry as Fran Quinn. No one has benefitted more poets, with his diligence, his warm heart, and his inventiveness."

One of the founders of the Worcester County Poetry Association in 1971, he organized Robert Bly's Mother Conference for years. In addition to teaching creative writing for over twenty-five years, he was the poet-in-residence and director of the internationally known Visiting Writers Series at Butler University, Indianapolis, Indiana for fifteen years, a series that brought in 500 poets worldwide. He now conducts regular poetry workshops in Indianapolis, Chicago, New York City, and elsewhere. Visit his website at franquinnworkshops.com.